THE POCKET BOOK OF

Fighters

THE POCKET BOOK OF
Fighters

MARTIN BOWMAN

The Definitive Guide to the Fighters of the World

BARNES & NOBLE BOOKS

NEW YORK

This edition published by Barnes & Noble, Inc.,
by arrangement with Salamander Books Ltd.

2004 Barnes and Noble Books

ISBN 0-7607-5888-3

© Salamander Books Ltd., 2004

An imprint of **Chrysalis** Books Group

A CIP catalog record for this book is available from the
Library of Congress.

CREDITS
Editor: Shaun Barrington
Designer: John Heritage
Reproduction: Anorax Imaging Ltd.
Production: Don Campaniello

Printed in India

Front cover: Grumman F-14 Tomcat. **Back cover:** Lockheed P-38, P-51B
Mustang, and P-47 Thunderbolt.
Page 1: The first Messerschmitt 262-A1 to be captured by U.S. troops
in World War II. **Page 2:** McDonnell Douglas AV-8B Harrier II Night
Attack, with AGM-65 Maverick air-to-surface guided missiles under the
wings. **Page 3:** MiG-29 "Fulcrum."

Contents

Introduction

The changing role of the fighter

Left: Birth of a legend.
RAF Duxford, where 19
Squadron shows off its
new Spitfire Is to the
press on May 4, 1939.

What is a fighter aircraft? In 1914 aircraft were mostly unarmed "scouts," or reconnaissance platforms, but by early 1915 two-seat designs were expected to fly in every role necessary for support of the ground war on the Western Front. Machine guns that could fire through the propeller arc were the height of technology and aerial duels or "dog-fights" were considered a chivalrous pursuit. Airmen who lived long enough to shoot down five enemy aircraft became aces, a term that persists in spite of fire-and-forget missiles and stand-off weapons. Despite an increasing reliance on technology, the fighter pilots' credo, "kill or be killed" remains as true today as it did in World War One. Despite radar and computerized gunsights, the mark one eyeball is still an essential means of staying alive in combat.

In The U.S. in the 1930s and 1940s fighters were officially known as "pursuits" while in the Navy "attack" planes and "scout bombers" were armed with guns, bombs and torpedoes, and Boeing and Curtiss fighter types were redesignated BF (bomber fighter) types. Germany decisively used air power in the Blitzkrieg, or lightning war of 1939–1940, when first Poland, then Norway, the Low Countries, and France quickly succumbed to the co-ordinated use of land, sea, and air forces. Aviation units alone could not possibly turn the tide, although there were

Above: Hurricane and Spitfire in formation.

Left: P-51Ds of the 361st Fighter Group, 8th Air Force, with D-Day invasion stripes, in formation.

some notable victories. May 10, 1940, is believed to have seen the worst losses suffered by an air force in a single day's operation, when the Luftwaffe lost 304 aircraft and 51 were damaged during the invasion of the Netherlands and Belgium. A Dutch force of Fokker D XXI fighters shot down 39 Ju 52 transports.

The Battle of Britain 1940 was a series of skirmishes and engagements; history would have been very different had it not been for the British integrated system of radar and the pilots of RAF Fighter Command. British aircraft losses were made good, and the U.S., although not yet in the war, helped. Seven different fighter types were in mass production in U.S. factories. The Curtiss P-40 was the first available in large numbers and during 1940–42 more P-40s were built than all other major fighter types combined. Pure fighters armed with cannon, bombs and rockets became fighter-bombers or were used as escorts for bombers. During 1942–45 the USAAF pursued a policy of daylight precision bombing of Germany, but heavy losses soon revealed a desperate need for escort fighters like the P-38, P-47, and P-51. At night RAF and *Nachtjagd* fighter crews waged a technological cat-and-mouse war over the Reich. Allied air forces eventually imposed total air superiority and in May 1945 Germany surrendered. Japan followed suit in August although only after the two atomic bombs had destroyed Hiroshima and Nagasaki. The nuclear era had dawned. Did this mean the end of the

fighter's conventional role? The last sixty years have shown this quite clearly not to have been the case.

The buzzword now was "all-weather," fighters that could operate by day and by night in any elements. The Curtiss XF-87 Blackhawk jet fighter, which first flew in March 1948, was the first aircraft built for this purpose. The Northrop F-89 Scorpion became the most successful long-range all-weather fighter, while the Lockheed F-94 was the first all-weather jet fighter in air force service. (In June 1948 the U.S. P-pursuit designation finally changed to F-fighter designation).

Cold War between the Western democracies and the Soviet Union and mutually assured destruction not surprisingly concentrated almost all attention on bombers rather than fighters. Not until the unexpected detonation of the first Soviet atomic bomb on August 29, 1949 did fighter production reach significant numbers again. One means of defense against Soviet bomber attack was the rocket-armed fighter. The F-86D Sabre was the first interceptor designed to carry air-to-air rockets and in late 1949 it became the first single-seat all-weather jet fighter in the world. Offensive or "penetration" fighters like the McDonnell XF-88, Lockheed XGF-90, and the F-86C were also developed. The first fighter designed for supersonic speeds was the Republic XF-91 interceptor, which first flew on May 9, 1949. In January 1951 design work began on the F-100, the first supersonic aircraft in the world to enter production. In the early 1950s Convair developed the next "century series" interceptor (F-102A) as part of a "weapons system" consisting of air-to-air guided missiles, all-weather radar search and fire control, and the supersonic single-seat fighter.

Left: BAe Harrier of No.1 Squadron, the world's first successful VTOL aircraft. Six of the squadron's GR3s sailed to the Falklands on May 7, 1982 on board the merchant vessel the *Atlantic Conveyor*. The next day 20 Harriers took off for the nine-hour flight.

On August 12, 1953, the Soviets tested a hydrogen bomb and on May 1, 1954 the prototype of the Mya-4 "Bison" jet bomber appeared. It set alarm bells ringing in the west. The U.S. pursued a policy of building more powerful supersonic fighters like the F-104, F-105, and F-106, to counter what was perceived (wrongly) as a growing fleet of Soviet intercontinental bombers with enough thermonuclear weapons to devastate targets in the continental U.S. and western Europe.

In Britain in April 1957 Duncan Sandys, the Minister of Defence, forecast the end of manned combat aircraft and their replacement by missiles. On November 25, 1958 the English Electric P.1B prototype became the first British aircraft to fly at Mach 2.

In the 1960s the McDonnell F-4 Phantom successfully initiated the era of the Mach 2 missile-launching fighter and became the most widely used U.S. supersonic fighter. NATO, meanwhile, pursued a "trip wire" policy, whereby conventional forces would precede all-out atomic warfare.

In Korea 1950-53 and Southeast Asia 1965-73, U.S. fighter-bombers were used very effectively as "strike" aircraft. Soviet fighter progress in the late 1960s, however, prompted a need for air superiority fighters capable of meeting the variable-sweep Mig-23 and the MiG-25 aircraft in combat. In 1974 the F-14 Tomcat, missile-armed and with the maneuverability to destroy enemy fighters in combat, became the first U.S. Navy carrier fighter in squadron service for 12 years. The F-15 Eagle, which appeared in 1972, was the first USAF fighter for many years to be designed purely for the air superiority role. Several NATO air forces and the USAF ordered the F-16, the first of the significant lightweight, low-cost, highly maneuverable fighters with Mach 2-speed capability.

In 1988 existence of the F-1117A Stealth, the production combat type designed to exploit low observable (LO) technology was officially revealed. Stealth technology fighters and conventional aircraft such as the F-15 and F-16 were used to great effect in the Gulf Wars of 1991 and 2003. For the foreseeable future high-technology "air dominance" fighters like the F-22 Raptor, the Eurofighter, and the F35A Joint Strike Fighter, will counter multiple defense threats, provide the air-defense mission, and protect fleet assets from airborne intruders.

Left: The USAF has plans for a fleet of 339 Raptors with a requirement for at least 381: but the spiralling costs imply that the Air Force can only now afford 218. Other nations have signed letters of intent, but how much they will contribute to the estimated $71 billion bill has not been confirmed.

Fighters 1939-45

Fast developments for a new battlefield

Left: Gloster Gladiator I. This remarkable, sturdy biplane fighter served with the RAF and twelve other air forces. It first entered RAF service in February 1937, and in 1940 fought valiantly against the Luftwaffe in Norway, destroying 36 enemy aircraft for the loss of only two in combat. In mid-June 1940 six Gladiators constituted the entire air defense of Malta. The Gladiator's greatest successes were against the *Regia Aeronautica* in Greece prior to the Luftwaffe's involvement. By the end of 1940 Flight Lieutenant M. T. St. J. Pattle DFC is known to have shot down at least 24 enemy aircraft in a Gladiator while flying from bases in Greece.

By the late 1930s many of the monoplane fighters that would become famous in WWII had all already flown. In 1935 the Messerschmitt Bf 109, the Curtiss Hawk 75, and Hawker Hurricane prototypes all flew. It is thought that 35,000 Bf 109s were built, while deliveries of P-40 versions reached 13,738 examples. In 1936 the Supermarine Spitfire and Messerschmitt Bf 110 day/night fighter prototypes made their maiden flights. In 1937 the revolutionary but ineffectual Boulton Paul Defiant gun turreted fighter prototype, and the Hawker Hurricane I production model, flew for the first time. In 1938 the Spitfire Mk.I production fighter, probably the most famous fighter name of the war, first flew. Total Spitfire production eventually reached 20,334 aircraft and 2,556 Seafire naval fighters were also built.

At the outbreak of war Luftwaffe fighter units were equipped with just over one thousand Bf 109Es. After meeting ineffectual opposition in the early offensives against Poland, the Low Countries, and France, it was not until late May 1940, over the beaches of Dunkirk, that the Bf 109E engaged in combat for the first time with its equal, the Spitfire. In combat, the 109E's greatest advantage over the Hurricane and Spitfire was the ability to perform negative-G maneuvers on account of its fuel-injection system. The

Above: Messerschmitt Bf 109G; the Bf 109 was responsible for destroying more enemy aircraft by day than any other aircraft in history.

Left: It was powered by a Daimler-Benz DB 605AM inverted V-12 piston engine, capable of developing 1,800hp with water/methanol injection.

RAF fighters were equipped with conventional carburetors and their Merlin engines lost power in negative-g conditions. Like the Spitfire, the Bf 109E had ground handling problems because of its narrow track landing gear and it tended to swing alarmingly on take-off and landing. Despite these and other problems, not least bad visibility from the cramped cockpit, the Bf 109E remained the Luftwaffe's first-line fighter until 1941, when the Bf 109F entered service.

The Hurricane was the most famous in the long line of Hawker single-seat fighters which, together with the Spitfire, was responsible for the defeat of the Luftwaffe in the Battle of Britain. Both British fighters were armed with eight .303 inch machine guns in the wings, a new innovation. In the 1930s these had been adapted from the U.S. Colt .300 Browning machine-gun to fire .303 rimless caliber ammunition and the gun was manufactured under license in Britain. Although the Hurricane was fabric-

covered, its construction was tubular steel and it proved easier to build than the Spitfire, which used a metal stressed-skin monocoque structure with only the control surfaces being fabric-covered. By September 1939, 497 Hurricanes had been built and by August 7, 1940, 2,309

Left: The Messerschmitt Bf 109 was one of the most famous fighters in history. Before the war Willie Messerschmitt's nimble little fighter already had a claim to fame. On November 11, 1937, a Bf 109 raised the landplane world speed record to 379.38 mph using a boosted DB 601 engine of 1,650 hp.

Above: Song of the Merlin. The mighty Rolls-Royce Merlin XX engine rated at 1,280 hp, at full revs during a ground test of a Hurricane IIC.

Hurricanes had been delivered (against 1,383 Spitfires). By early August 1940, the Hurricane equipped 32 squadrons in the RAF and the Spitfire equipped 18$\frac{1}{2}$ squadrons. In the Battle of Britain the Hurricane was flown by about six in every ten squadrons and it accounted for more enemy aircraft destroyed than any other type of British aircraft. By the end of the Battle of Britain the Hurricane had shot down more than 1,500 enemy aircraft. Total Hurricane production eventually reached 12,780 in Britain and 1,451 in Canada and the aircraft served on no fewer than 17 different fronts.

Above: Spitfires of the Battle of Britain Memorial Flight in formation. Evaluation of a Bf 109E-3 captured in France in 1940 revealed that the German fighter was superior to the Spitfire I in several respects: it was faster at most altitudes and better in the dive.

The Spitfire was the most famous aircraft ever to see service with the RAF and was the only Allied fighter to remain in continuous production throughout the war. In all, 27 different marks saw service up until 1947 and total Spitfire/Seafire production reached 22,759. Numerically, the Mark V was the most important Spitfire produced, with a total of 6,479. As the RAF turned to the offensive the Spitfire V was developed to enable Fighter Command to retain its initiative over the Messerschmitt Bf 109. Intended initially as a stop-gap, the Mk V was basically a Mk I or II structurally strengthened to accommodate the

Right: ECFS Spitfire Is and Hurricane I on September 16, 1942.

Below: Bell XP-59A Airacomet. In September 1941 Bell Aircraft Corporation undertook development of a jet-fighter to take advantage of early British design work on gas-turbine power plants. The P-59As were followed by P-59Bs before the contract was cancelled in October 1943 because of the successful development of the P-80.

Left: Hurricane IICs in formation. Sydney Camm's immortal design, like that of Leslie Mitchell's at Vickers Supermarine, was altered on the drawing board with the decision in January 1934 to proceed with the new Rolls-Royce PV12 engine (the Merlin) in place of the steam-cooled in-line Goshawk engine. The prototype Hurricane flew on November 6, 1935. In June 1936 "Scheme F" called for the production of 500 Hurricanes within three years and an order for a further 400 was issued in November 1938. The first production Hurricane differed from the prototype in having a 1,030 hp Rolls-Royce Merlin II engine, modified cockpit canopy and exhaust pipes, and a re-designed undercarriage fairing. In 1939 metal-covered wings began to replace the fabric-covered wings in production.

heavier and more powerful Rolls-Royce 1,470 hp Merlin 45 vee-12 engine. Another important difference between the Mk II and the Mk V was the introduction of metal ailerons over the former's fabric type. Rate of roll at high speeds was doubled. The Mark VA still carried eight .303 in. Browning machine-guns but the VB housed two 20-mm

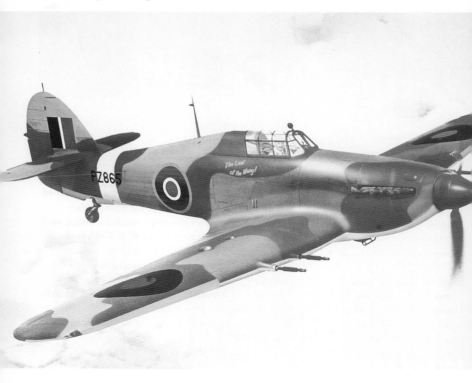

Above: The Mustang was designed from the outset to meet British requirements as a long-range wing mate for the Spitfire and Hurricane. The P-51B pictured was powered by the Merlin.

Left: Hawker Hurricane IIC PZ865 *The Last of the Many!* This aircraft was the 12,780th and final Hurricane built and was delivered in September 1944.

cannon and four machine-guns. The Mark VC introduced a "universal" wing capable of housing eight machine-guns, or two cannon and four machine-guns, or four cannon. Alternatively, a drop tank or 500-lb bomb could be carried under the center fuselage. In Europe the Spitfire V's ascendancy over the Luftwaffe pretty much continued until the autumn of 1941, when the Focke Wulf 190A burst onto the scene over the coast of France. This German fighter was undoubtedly the most advanced in the world and completely out-classed the Spitfire V, except that the latter aircraft had a much better turning circle. Fortunately, the Luftwaffe failed to press home its new-found advantage, choosing to remain mainly on the defensive in the west in 1942.

On May 15, 1941 the de Havilland Mosquito night-fighter prototype flew for the first time and was designated

Left: Lockheed P-38, P-51B Mustang and P-47 Thunderbolt. The first unit to operate the P-38 was the 342nd Composite Group operating from Icelandic bases. The first German aircraft to be shot down by a USAAF fighter was an FW 200 Condor on August 12, 1942, by two P-38s from the 27th Squadron, 1st Fighter Group, and a P-40, near Iceland. The P-38's development as a long-range tactical fighter was delayed because of the prevailing belief that U.S. heavy bombers could defend themselves on long daylight missions over Europe; but in raids on the Reich 1943-45, P-38s, Mustangs, and Thunderbolts escorted the U.S. bombers to their targets and back.

Left and below right:
Republic P-43 Lancer, P-40
Warhawk (second from
camera and **below right**),
P-39 Airacobra, and P-38
Lightning. The P-43 was
was the world's first 300-
mph fighter and the first
all-metal pursuit plane
with semi-elliptical
fuselage. In 1937 the
USAAC contracted Bell
Aircraft Corporation to
build a single XP-39 high-
altitude pursuit interceptor
prototype. It was capable
of operating at 15,000 ft
and fired a nose-mounted
37-mm T-9 cannon through
the aircrew hub. The
cannon mounting dictated
the Allison V-1710 engine
position, buried in the
fuselage section aft of the
cockpit. The XP-39
prototype flew on April 6,
1939 and the P-39
Airacobra went into full
production in August 1939.

Mosquito II. The type was fitted with the then highly secret Al Mk IV airborne radar device for intercepting enemy bombers at night. The fighter variant of the Mosquito differed from the bomber variant in having strengthened wing spars to take the extra strain imposed by fighter maneuvers, and the nose was modified to house four 20 mm cannon and four machine-guns. A flat, bullet-proof windscreen was fitted and the two-man crew entered through a door on the starboard side of the fuselage instead of through a hatch in the floor, as on the bomber.

The Mosquito II first entered service with Fighter Command in January 1942. The most widely used of all the Mosquito fighters was the Mk VI fighter-bomber, which was developed as a result of the success gained by the Mosquito II night-intruder. Altogether, about 2,500 Mk VIs were built.

The Soviet Union's most numerous fighter was the Yakovlev YAK-1/3, reputedly based on the Supermarine Spitfire and Bf 109. The cockpit featured armored glass, which took the place of armor plate around the pilot's shoulder height. To its cost the Luftwaffe discovered that the Yak-3 was superior to the Bf 109G below 19,685 ft and it could turn inside the FW 190 fighter-bomber. Some 37,000 Yak-1, -3, -7 and -9 fighters were built.

Right: The P-38 Lightning was one of the most easily recognizable fighters of WWII and together with the P-47 and P-51, formed the mainstay of the U.S. fighter force in the USAAF 1941-45. Despite its drawbacks, the P-38's devastating firepower and excellent rate of climb earned the respect of its German adversaries, who referred to the P-38 as the "Fork-Tailed Devil."

Several promising U.S. fighters had been on the drawing board in the 1930s and fought in World War II. The P-38 Lightning was one of the most easily recognizable fighters of the war and together with the P-47 and P-51 formed the mainstay of the U.S. fighter force in the USAAF from 1941-45. Originally designed in 1937 as a high altitude interceptor, the P-38's development as a long-range tactical fighter was delayed because of the prevailing belief

Below: Design of the Soviet Polikarpov I-16 single seat radial-engined fighter began as far back as 1933. Over 270 I-16s were used in the Spanish Civil War. When German forces invaded in June 1941, almost two-thirds of the Soviet air force fighter arm consisted of I-16s and they remained in action until 1943.

that U.S. heavy bombers could defend themselves on long daylight missions over Europe. By mid-1942 when heavy losses in the bomber groups made it obvious that long-range escort fighters would, after all, be required, the P-38F began to be deployed in large numbers in the European Theater of Operations (ETO). Although slightly slower and less maneuverable than most single-engined fighters then in service, the Lightning's greater range made it an excellent escort fighter. It could take a great deal of punishment, lose one engine and still get its pilot home. The P-38J version appeared in August 1943 and was used mainly to accompany U.S. heavy bombers of the 8th and 15th Air Forces on long-range missions from Britain and

Below: The Northrop P-6l Black Widow was the first aircraft ever specifically designed as a night-fighter. The P-61 equipped eight squadrons in the Pacific from June 1944. Its retractable laminar flow ailerons and lateral-control spoilers allowed fast, tight turns to out-turn a Hellcat, and give even the Spitfire a run for its money.

Italy respectively. Beginning in November 1942, P-38s also saw service in significant numbers in North Africa and the Mediterranean theater. In combat with the Luftwaffe for the first time the Lightning gave a good account of itself. Despite its drawbacks, the P-38's devastating firepower and excellent rate of climb earned the respect of its German adversaries, who referred to the P-38 as the "Fork-Tailed Devil."

The P-51 Mustang also saw widespread use as an escort fighter on long-penetration raids deep inside Germany. The Mustang's range of 2,080 miles, achieved by the use of wing drop tanks, was far in excess of that available in other fighters of the day. By the end of the war

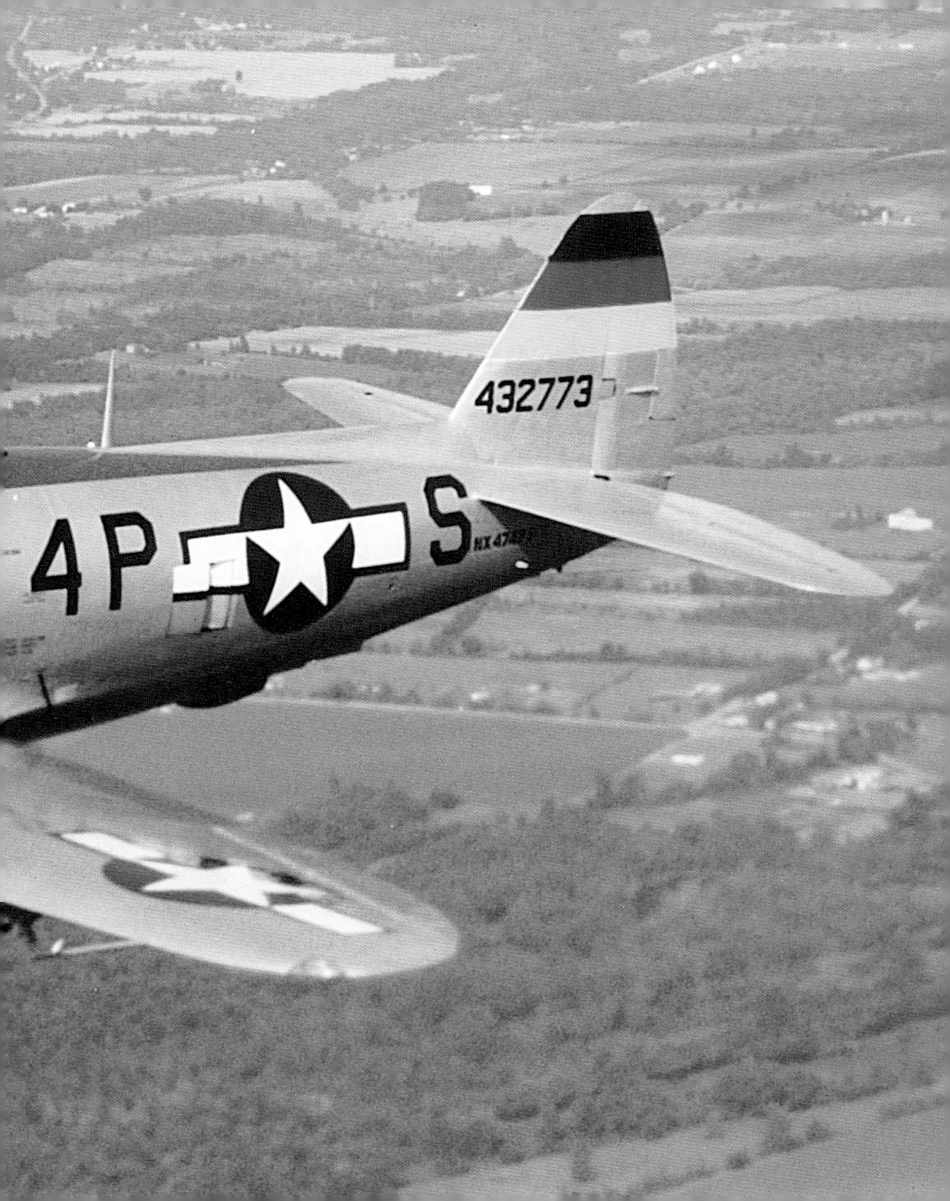
432773
4P S

Previous page: Republic P-47D Thunderbolt *Big Ass Bird II*. Designed originally as a strategic escort for deep penetration B-17s and B-24s over Europe, the P-47 also served with distinction in the Pacific. The fast-diving P-47 soon gained the healthy respect of its pilots.

Right: P-51D *Montana Miss* with *Kansas City Kitty* behind. The P-51B was followed by 1,750 P-51C variants, which had increased internal fuel capacity and a British-designed Malcolm bulged sliding hood. The P-51D introduced a streamlined bubble (teardrop) canopy with a lowered rear decking, and on later examples a change from four machine guns to six. Later, a dorsal fin fairing was added. The P-51D could carry two bombs of up to 1,000 lb and later versions were armed with six 5-in rockets.

the P-51 equipped all but one of the 8th Air Force fighter groups. The P-51B was followed by 1,750 P-51C variants, which had increased internal fuel capacity and a British-designed bulged sliding hood. With a maximum speed of

442 mph at 24,500 ft, it was more than a match for
German propeller fighters in 1944 and could operate far
over the continent with the aid of drop tanks. Mustangs
continued to escort medium and heavy bombers over the

Right: Wooden wonders! On November 25, 1940 the prototype Mosquito first flew and astounded everyone with a remarkable top speed of almost 400 mph and a display of superb maneuverability. The original contract for fifty bombers was changed to twenty bombers and thirty fighters. A night-fighter prototype was designated Mosquito II. The night-fighters were in wartime service for three years and at one time destroyed 1,200 enemy aircraft and V1s in sixty nights. Post-war, mostly the NF36 and NF38 night-fighter versions served with Fighter Command until the advent of the jet night-fighter in 1951. The NF38 was the last type to be produced. 7,781 Mosquitoes of 43 different operational marks were built in Britain, Canada and Australia.

continent in 1944 and later crossed to France with the 2nd Tactical Air Force to act as fighter-bombers. The P-51D introduced a streamlined bubble (teardrop) canopy and a change from four machine guns to six. Later, a dorsal fin fairing was added. The P-51D was the most successful of all the Mustang models and was built in greater quantity than any other variant. Altogether, some 7,956 Ds were built and the type first saw service in Europe in 1944 with the USAAF and RAF.

Designed originally as a strategic escort for deep penetration B-17s and B-24s over Europe, the P-47 also served with distinction in the Pacific. Early models were known as "Razorbacks" because of their raised rear fuselage leading to the framed cockpit hood. The first P-47Ds retained this canopy but from P-47D-25 on, Thunderbolts were fitted with a "teardrop" molded cockpit hood for improved rearward vision. Altogether, some 12,602 'Ds were built. By February 1943, both the 56th and 78th Fighter Groups of the 8th Air Force in England were operational on the P-47C and P-47D. Known alternatively as the "Flying Milk Bottle" because of its shape and "Jug" (for Juggernaut) because of its ability to out-dive any other fighter, the P-47 soon gained the respect of its pilots. P-47s flew their first escort mission on May 4, 1943, when they accompanied B-17s to Antwerp. After early teething troubles the P-47's value as a long-range escort was proved when two 150-gallon drop tanks were fitted below the wings to enable the P-47 to fly all the way to the target. By August 1945 P-47s had flown on every front, destroying over 7,000 enemy aircraft on the ground and in the air. Altogether, 15,660 Thunderbolts were built and the last were phased out of service in 1955.

In the Pacific, USAAC, U.S. Navy, USMC, and Royal Naval fighters fought over land and sea. The Air Corps' P-38 Lightning destroyed more Japanese aircraft than any other U.S. aircraft and the two leading U.S. aces, Major Richard Bong and Major Tom McGuire (40 and 38 kills respectively), flew P-38s in the Pacific theater. In April

1943 Lightnings of the 339th Fighter Squadron succeeded in intercepting and shooting down the Mitsubishi transport carrying Admiral Yamamoto, mastermind of the Japanese attack on Pearl Harbor, December 7, 1941. The interception, 550 miles from base at Guadalcanal, was made possible by the use of long-range drop tanks.

Left: P-51D Mustangs of the 352nd Fighter Group, 8th Air Force at Bodney, England, in the summer of 1945. The Group was known as the Blue Nosed B...ds of Bodney, for obvious reasons.

The P-51D also saw escort duty in the Pacific. In February 1945 P-51Ds flying from Iwo Jima escorted B-29s to attack Japan. On April 7 P-51Ds penetrated Tokyo airspace for the first time. A few P-51H models reached the Pacific before the end of the War and served operationally. This was the fastest of all Mustangs, having a top speed of 487 mph. Some 830 P-47 Thunderbolts served with 16 RAF squadrons in Burma up until VJ-Day. The final Thunderbolt models were the P-47M, of which 130 were built by 1945, and the P-47N, built solely for the Pacific Theatre. It had an 18-inch greater span than the P-47M to accommodate two 93-gallon tanks in addition to two drop tanks. With internal fuselage tanks and a 100-gallon belly drop tank, the P-47N had a range of 2,350 miles. Nearing the end of the war P-47Ns flew escort for the B-29s bombing targets in Japan.

The first in the famous line of Grumman-built naval fighters was the F-4F Wildcat, which was the U.S. Navy's

Right: Although slower than other U.S. fighters and out-performed by the Japanese Zero, in the Pacific theater the Grumman F4F Wildcat averaged almost seven enemy aircraft shot down to every one F4F lost. This can be attributed to its rugged construction and the skill of its pilots. One of the most memorable feats attributed to this aircraft occurred on February 20, 1942. USN Lt Cdr Edward "Butch" O'Hare single-handedly saved his carrier, *Lexington*, by breaking up an attack of nine Japanese bombers and shooting down five of them in six minutes. O'Hare became one of the first U.S. aces and was awarded the Medal of Honor. Altogether, some 8,000 Wildcats were built from 1939 to 1942.

Left: P-40 and P-47. The final Thunderbolt models were the P-47M, of which 130 were built by 1945, and the P-47N, built solely for the Pacific theater. It had an 18-inch greater span than the P-47M for two 93-gallon tanks in addition to two-drop tanks. With internal fuselage tanks and a 100-gallon belly drop tank, the P-47N had a range of 2,350 miles. Nearing the end of the war P-47Ns flew escort for the B-29s bombing targets in Japan. By August 1 945 P-47s had flown on every front destroying over 7,000 enemy aircraft on the ground and in the air.

Below: Restored F6F-5K B showing the famous "Felix the Cat" emblem of Fighting Squadron Six and the Japanese flag symbols that represent nine of Lt (jg) Alexander Vraciu's victories gained flying F6F-5Ks with VF-6.

Left: Commander David McCampbell, Commander Air Group 15, USS *Essex* in F6F-5 *Minsi III*. On October 24, 1944, the opening day of the Battle of Leyte Gulf, McCampbell, assisted by just one other Hellcat, attacked a formation of 60 fighters, shooting down nine of them, completely disorganizing the enemy group and forcing the remainder to abandon their attack on the task force before a single aircraft could reach the fleet. For this action, the destruction of another seven in one day, June 19, 1944, and his inspired leadership of Air Group 15, McCampbell was awarded the Medal of Honor. Twice an ace in a day, McCampbell was the top-scoring naval pilot in World War Two, with 34 confirmed victories.

standard carrier-borne fighter, 1941-1943. Although slower than other U.S. fighters and out-performed by the Japanese Zero, the Wildcat averaged almost seven enemy aircraft shot down to every one F4F lost. Altogether, some 8,000 Wildcats were built from 1939 to 1942. The Mitsubishi A6M Zero-Sen (Type 00 fighter) was designed in 1937 and flew for the first time in April 1939. The type entered production as the A6M2 Reisen in 1940. Its first combat test occurred in July 1940 during the Sino-Japanese War, where it out-performed all other types in combat used in China, including the Curtiss P-40s of Claire Chennault's Flying Tigers U.S. volunteer force. The highly maneuverable and heavily armed A6M2 Zero was superior to the F4F Wildcat and even to U.S. land-based fighters, but it was poorly armored and in combat its light alloy construction tended to catch fire easily. U.S. Navy F4F pilots soon learned to avoid close-in dog-fights with the Zero and used their superior diving speeds instead.

During 1942–43 F4U Corsairs and F6F Hellcats achieved air superiority. By October 1944 the Imperial Navy had lost its aircraft carriers and The Zero finished the war as a land-based fighter. Few experienced Japanese fighter pilots remained to fly them, so they were used on Kamikaze suicide missions against Allied shipping. The A6M5 was the largest quantity Zero produced and by the end of the war some 10,937 Zeros of all types had been built.

The Vought F4U Corsair or "Whistling Death" as the Japanese called it, was by far the finest carrier-borne fighter of World War II. It was the first U.S. Navy fighter to exceed 400 mph in level flight and of all the fighters built during the war the F4U was to remain in production

Right: Like most Grumman fighters the Hellcat's claim to fame lies in the Pacific. It was designed as a replacement for the Grumman Wildcat in U.S. Navy service and first flew on June 26, 1942. The F6F first entered combat with VF-5 of USS *Yorktown* and VF-9 of USS *Essex* on 31 August 1943 with strikes against Marcus Island. The Hellcat showed a marked superiority against Japanese aircraft, serving with the majority of U.S. Navy and Marine Corps squadrons in the Pacific. By the close of 1943 about 2,500 Hellcats had been delivered to operational squadrons. Almost 75 percent of all the U.S. Navy's air-to-air victories were attributed to the F6F, with a ratio of 19:1, destroying 4,947 enemy aircraft, plus another 209 claimed by land-based units.

the longest. Among its other many claims to fame was its 11:1 ratio of kills to losses in combat against Japanese aircraft. When the production model appeared in June 1942 its far-aft cockpit and inverted gull wings represented an unorthodox design but its greatest attribute was its excellent overall performance, which was achieved by simply designing the smallest possible airframe around the most powerful engine. However, deck-landing trials with the U.S. Navy revealed that the F-4U's long nose ahead of

the cockpit made it difficult for pilots to see the landing
signal officer (LSO). For this reason the first F-4Us were
used as land-based fighters. Deliveries of the F4U-l to the
U.S. Marine Corps began in October 1942 and the type
was first used in action by the "Cactus Air Force" during
the defense of Guadalcanal from Japanese air, ground, and
sea assaults in February 1943. It was not until 1944 that
the F-4U was finally deemed ready for U.S. carrier-based
operations. Improvements to the cockpit included a raised

Right: The P-38 destroyed more Japanese aircraft than any other U.S. aircraft and the two leading U.S. aces, Major Richard Bong and Major Tom McGuire (40 and 38 kills respectively), flew P-38s in the Pacific theater. A Lightning is on display at Oshkosh in the colors of Major Bong's P-38 *Marge*. In April 1943 Lightnings of the 339th Fighter Squadron succeeded in intercepting and shooting down the Mitsubishi transport carrying Admiral Yamamoto, mastermind of the Japanese attack on Pearl Harbor. The interception, 550 miles from their base at Guadalcanal, was made possible by the use of long-range drop tanks. When production ended in 1945, almost 10,000 P-38s had been built.

pilot's seat and a large single-piece canopy, while pilots perfected a new landing approach, often with their port wing slightly down so that the LSO could be kept in sight. In fact the Fleet Air Arm were the first to use Corsairs at sea, on April 3, 1944, when British carrier-borne aircraft attacked the German battleship Tirpitz. The F-4U fought in every major Pacific battle with the U.S. Navy, flying 64,051 sorties and destroying 2,140 Japanese aircraft with the loss of only 189 of its number.

The F-6F Hellcat was designed as a replacement for the Wildcat in U.S. Navy service and first flew on June 26, 1942. The F6F first entered combat on August 31, 1943, with strikes against Marcus Island. From then on the Hellcat showed a marked superiority against Japanese aircraft, serving with the majority of U.S. Navy and Marine Corps squadrons in the Pacific theater. By the close of 1943 approximately 2,500 Hellcats had been delivered

Above: The Japanese Zero was the finest of all Japanese fighters of World War II, but one of the best all-round fighters in the Pacific was the Kawanishi N12-J Shiden-Kai George 21 (on display at the Air Force Museum, Dayton, Ohio), produced during the last year of the war. Only 428 were built because of initial production problems and later shortages of parts resulting from B-29 raids on Japan.

to operational squadrons. Almost 75 percent of all the U.S. Navy's air-to-air victories were attributed to the F6F, with a ratio of 19:1, destroying 4,947 enemy aircraft plus another 209 claimed by land-based units. The pinnacle of its glittering Pacific career was reached during the Battle of the Philippine Sea (19–20 June 1944) when the Hellcat effectively halted the Japanese attack on the first day, accounting for most of the 300 aircraft lost by the Japanese Air Force. By the end of 1944 some six squadrons of FAA Hellcats were in service with the British Pacific Fleet, seeing action off Malaya. In January 1945 Hellcats took part in the large-scale raids on Japanese oil refineries, at Pangkalan Brandan and Palembang. By August 1946 the type had been phased out of FAA service, most having been returned to the U.S. under the terms of Lend-Lease. By the time production ceased in November 1945, some 12,275 Hellcats had been produced.

From Pistons to Jets
Rockets, records, and Korea

The U.S. benefited greatly from German wartime aeronautical research and from the British lead in jet engine and carrier technology. As early as 1937, Frank (later Sir Frank) Whittle had run the first gas turbine aero engine in Britain. In 1943 the Miles M-52 had been the first research aircraft to be designed for flight at 1,000 mph. Detailed design was virtually complete by 1946 when the project was cancelled, but models flown during 1947-48 proved that the turbojet-powered aircraft would have achieved 1,000 mph. Britain's first operational jet fighter, the Gloster Meteor Mk I, entered squadron service in July 1944. The first production Meteor Mk I was sent to the U.S. in February 1944 in exchange for a Bell YP-59 Airacomet as part of an Anglo-American agreement reached in mid-1943.

On November 7, 1945 a Meteor F.4 of the High Speed Flight had established a New World Air Speed Record of 606 mph. On September 7, 1946 Britain increased the record to 616 mph. A Rolls-Royce 5,000-lb thrust Nene centrifugal-flow turbojet was installed in the first Grumman XF9F-2, which flew on August 16, 1948. Early production MiG-15s, the result of a Soviet project in 1946 that benefited from German research into swept wings, were powered by the same engine, sold to the Soviets under the Anglo-Soviet Trade Agreement of 1946. *(Cont. page 60)*

Above: The Grumman F8F Bearcat was designed to replace the F6F and operate from even the smallest of carriers to help combat the Japanese Kamikaze aircraft in the Pacific war. However, it only began replacing the Hellcat in fleet service in 1945, when F8F-1s were embarked aboard the light carrier *Langley* with VF-19, but the war ended before combat deployment in the Pacific, by which time only 151 examples had been built.

Left: *Gulfhawk IV*, a G-58A (civil version of the F8F-1) powered by a 2,100 hp Pratt & Whitney Double Wasp CA-15 18-cylinder radial, ordered for Major Al Williams of the Gulf Oil Company, first flew on July 23, 1947. It was later re-registered NL3025, but shortly afterward was destroyed in a landing accident at Elizabeth, New Jersey.

Right: Lavochkin La-9 "Fritz" (La-130) a development of the World War II La-5/La-7 series designed as an escort fighter to accompany Tu-2 bombers. The La-130 prototype was completed in 1946. A long-range escort version of the La-9 was also developed under the designation La-11 "Fang," and this differed in having all-metal construction.

Above: The Gloster Meteor first flew on March 5, 1943, and was the only Allied jet to see operational service in World War II. The Meteor gave Britain a world lead in jet-powered aircraft, which was not seriously challenged by the U.S. until 1947. This is a Meteor III.

The U.S. did not seriously challenge Britain's world lead in jet fighter design until June 1947 when the Lockheed P-80R Shooting Star captured the World Air Speed Record flying at a speed of 623.74 mph. Later that same year the Douglas Skystreak raised it even further, to 650.92 mph. The F-86 Sabre, America's first supersonic jet fighter, was one of several immediate post-war aircraft to benefit from German wartime research and the Sabre's straight wing was soon replaced by a swept-wing design. In March 1948 the navalized version, the FJ-l Fury, became the first USN jet fighter to go to sea under operational

Above: The rocket-powered Bell X-1 was the first aircraft to fly faster than the speed of sound on October 14, 1947, at the hands of Captain Charles "Chuck" Yeager. Pictured is the Bell X-1E 46-063 *Little Joe*. Joe Walker made a total of 21 flights as the X-1E project.

conditions. Britain no longer ruled the waves, but every innovation aboard carriers, including the angled flight deck, the steam catapult, and the mirror landing sight, was British-inspired.

After the defeat of Japan and with the onset of the Cold War the U.S. military found a role in Europe when in 1946 chilly relations with the Soviets and the eastern bloc showed the first signs of freezing over. On September 18, 1947 the USAF became a separate service. On June 24, 1948 the Soviets closed all the border routes to East Germany. Berlin was totally isolated. Over two million

Previous page: An April 1944 order for 200 Hawker Furies for the RAF was cancelled at the end of the war, though development of the Sea Fury for the Fleet Air Arm continued. The prototype flew in February 1945. Main variant was the Sea Fury FB.Mk.11, of which 615 examples were built, No.802 Squadron being the first unit to receive the type, in May 1948. Within this total were 66 FB.Mk.11s for the Royal Australian and Royal Canadian navies. These are Netherlands AFB.50s.

Right: Development of the Supermarine Swift began in 1946 as a replacement for the Gloster Meteor. It was unsuitable as an interceptor and it was restricted to the tactical reconnaissance role. F.7 versions (F.7 XF114 pictured) had a larger nose to accommodate radar.

people of the American, French and British zones of Berlin were almost entirely reliant upon food supplies form the West. So on June 26 the Berlin Airlift began. 500,000 tons of foodstuffs and 1.5 million tons of coal were flown in. The Soviet Union capitulated on May 16, 1949 and the borders were reopened. The signing of the North Atlantic

Pact established NATO on April 4, 1950. In December that year the NATO Council appointed Gen. Dwight D. Eisenhower as the first Supreme Allied Commander Europe (SACEUR), and on Christmas Day the U.S. Government announced that its military forces in Europe were at the disposal of the NATO command.

John Derry in the De Havilland DH 108 made the first British supersonic flight during a dive on September 9, 1948. It was also the first jet aircraft in the world to exceed Mach 1 (about 760 mph at sea level). It was not until September 1953 that Britain, with the Hawker Hunter 3, recaptured the World Air Speed Record and that same month the Supermarine Swift 4 increased it to 735.70 mph. The Douglas F4D-I Skyray enjoyed a brief claim to fame when

Left: In January 1951 the Armstrong-Whitworth Meteor NF.11 entered service with No.29 Squadron at RAF Tangmere. Prior to this the wartime Mosquito night-fighter remained Britain's only air defense at night. All NF.11 and subsequent variants were characterized by the long span wing and elongated nose, which housed the interception radar. The Meteor NF.Mk.11 prototype first flew on May 31, 1950 and the tropicalized version, the Meteor NF.13, first flew on December 23, 1952. The Meteor NF.Mk.12 differed in having a higher limiting Mach number and American-built APS-81 radar. Altogether, Meteor night-fighters equipped twelve squadrons in Fighter Command.

Left: North American F-82G Twin Mustang with SCR-720 radar pod of the 347th Fighter Group in Japan in 1949–50. It looks like two Mustang fuselages on one wing, but it was a totally new design, to allow room for a co-pilot/navigator on long-range bomber escort missions. During the Korean War, Japan-based F-82s were among the first USAF aircraft to operate over Korea. The first three North Korean airplanes destroyed by U.S. forces were shot down by all-weather F-82G interceptors on June 27, 1950.

Left: The de Havilland Vampire prototype flew at Hatfield on September 20, 1943 powered by a 2,700 lb thrust DH Goblin 1 turbojet. Vampire F.1s entered RAF service in April 1946. The 1946 F.3 differed from the F.1 in having increased fuel tankage in the wings and a redesigned tail assembly. The 1948 FB.5 was operated by the FEAF (Far East Air Force) against Malayan terrorists, and replaced earlier marks in the UK and RAF Germany. Vampires were widely exported and built under license.

Below: Royal Navy Blackburn Firebrand, first used as a short-range interceptor and later a torpedo carrying strike fighter. Too late for WWII, the final Firebrand Mks 5 and 5A entered service with No. 813 Squadron in April 1947.

Right: P-80C-5-LO 47-590 *Butch* of the 45th Tactical Reconnaissance Squadron —"Flying Polkadots"—at Misawa AFB, Japan, at the time of the Korean War. The Lockheed F-80 Shooting Star saw action in Korea first as a fighter, then as a fighter-bomber, until it was replaced by the F-86 and F-84. In 1951 70 F-80As were modified to reconnaissance configuration.

Right: At the start of the war in Korea many of the 1,804 Mustangs with the ANG and in storage were put back into service and within a year three USAF wings were serving in Korea. By the end of the conflict the F-51 had flown 62,607 sorties, primarily in the ground support role, for the loss of 194 aircraft. The Mustang pictured is an RF-51D in Japan at the time of the Korean War.

Lt-Cdr James B. Verdin USN eclipsed this record within a month with a speed of 752.94 mph. The record stood for 25 days. In October Lt-Col. Frank Everest USAF set a record of 755 mph in an F-100 Super Sabre, the first of the U.S. "Century Series" of fighter aircraft. In August 1955 Col Harold Hanes USAF set the first supersonic air speed record, also in an F-100. U.S. fighters went on to all but dominate supersonic flight.

As the Cold War intensified, military confrontation between east and west finally came. (*Cont. page 78*)

Left: Republic F-84G-15 Thunderjet 51-1199 fighter-bomber of the 49th FBW in Japan at the time of the Korean War. In all 3,025 F-84Gs were built, 1,936 of which served in NATO air forces.

Previous page: Lockheed F-94A Starfires entered service with the 319th All-Weather Fighter Squadron, 325th FIG in CONAC (Continental Air Command, from 1951 Air Defense Command)) in June 1950. Only five Starfire squadrons operated outside the mainland U.S., two in Korea where at first they operated well behind the front line to avoid their top secret radar equipment falling into enemy hands. From 1952 onwards Starfires were used as escort fighters on night raids with B-29s.

Right: RF-80C 44-85260 *Miss Carole B*, one of seventy F-80A-1s modified in 1951 to reconnaissance configuration, of the 45th Tactical Reconnaissance Squadron at Misawa, Japan, during the Korean War.

In Korea on June 25, 1950, the North Korean Army crossed the 38th Parallel, completely wrong-footing the South and its U.S. advisors. The North enjoyed total air superiority from the outset, but U.S. commanders had had

no reason to fear the Communist air threat because only piston-engined aircraft confronted them. USAF aircraft were ill suited to operate in a close air support and interdiction campaign in Korea. They needed paved

runways 6,000 ft long and these only existed in Japan, which meant that air operations over Korea were restricted to only a few minutes. U.S. and Royal Navy carriers, therefore, were essential during the long, grueling campaign, which was to last 38 months. Navy units could operate in the Sea of Japan and be sent off from about 70 miles from the coast of Korea. Royal Navy Sea Fury piston-engined fighters operated very successfully in the ground attack role during the early part of the war. On August 9, 1952 a Sea Fury flown by Lt P. Carmichael of 802 Squadron FAA destroyed a MiG-15 jet and on November 2, 1952 the first jet night kill was made when a Douglas F3D-2 Skyknight shot down a Yak-15. On July 3, 1950 Grumman Panthers were the

Left: F4U-4s and Skyraiders of the USS *Philippine Sea* prior to a strike over Korea in 1951.

Left: F4U-4 Corsair "418/M" of VF-24 taxies away after landing on the USS *Philippine Sea* off Korea in 1951.

Below: F4U-5NL night-fighter Corsair of VC-3 all-weather combat fighter squadron, fitted with an APS-19 radar intercept scanner in a housing on the starboard wing. In July 1953, Lt Guy P. Bordelon Jr. and a fellow pilot of VC-3 aboard the USS *Princeton*, were dispatched to K-6 airfield south of Seoul to try to counter "Heckling" missions flown by NKAF Yak-18 training aircraft, which were proving more than just a nuisance to USMC operations. In three night missions over a three-week period Bordelon destroyed five "Bed Check Charlies," as they were known, to become the only Navy ace in Korea.

first jet fighters in the USN to go into action when 30 F9F-2s provided top cover for Skyraiders and F4U Corsairs that bombed targets near the North Korean capital, Pyongyang.

The war compelled the U.S. to strengthen its air and ground forces in Europe and the Far East. Many USAF types were used throughout the next three years of fighting, including F-80C Shooting Stars, F-82 Twin Mustangs, F-84s and F-86 Sabres. The overwhelming balance of air power changed dramatically with the intervention of Communist China and the appearance, on November 1, 1950, of Soviet-built MiG-15 jets in North Korean airspace. F-86A Sabres tussled with the MiGs for the first time on December 17. (*Cont. page 92*)

Right: The de Havilland Sea Venom was built under license by Fiat in Turin and in Switzerland and France. Four Sea Venom Mk20s, powered by Fiat-built Ghost 48 engines, were assembled in France by SNCA as SE Aquilon 20 prototypes (pictured), equivalent to the Sea Venom Mk 52 and first flown in February 1952. Sud-Est built 75 Aquilon 202s, 40 single-seat Aquilon 203s and the unarmed Aquilon 204 trainer for the French Naval Air Service.

Left: Grumman F9F-2 Panther jet in flight. A Rolls-Royce 5,000-lb thrust Nene was installed in the first Grumman XF9F-2, which first flew on November 24, 1947. The following XF9F-3 was powered by a 4,600-lb thrust Allison J33-A-8, similar in size to the Nene. Contracts for 47 F9F-2s with the Pratt & Whitney J42-P-6 version of the Nene and 54 F9Fpower-3s with Allison J33-A-8s followed. Since the powerplants were not interchangeable, after October 1949 all F9F-3s were converted to F9F-2s; 567 were built.

Below: 62. An F9F-2B Panther of VF-112 taxies in on *Philippine Sea* (CV-47). The Panther was to remain the USN's first-line jet fighter throughout the first year of the Korean War. Of the 826 USN and USMC jets deployed, no fewer than 715 were F9F-2s flying about 78,000 combat sorties. USMC Panthers flew missions from land bases.

Left: Grumman Panthers on the flight deck of the *Philippine Sea* as Douglas Skyraiders take off for another raid on Korea, 1951. Some 621 F9F-2s were built, followed by 109 F9F-4s and 595 F9F-5s. The Allison A33-A-16 used on the F9F-4 was replaced by a Pratt & Whitney J48-P-2 (modelled on the Rolls-Royce Tay) on the F9F-5, which differed from previous models in having a higher pointed tail. By December 1952, 619 F9F-5s had been accepted. The final production model of the Panther was the F9F-5P photo reconnaissance version, of which 36 were built. The last Panthers, operated by VMF(AW)-314 USMC, were withdrawn from service in 1957.

Left: The USN desperately needed to achieve performance parity with the MiG-15 in Korea, so swept wings and tail were added to the standard Grumman Panther fuselage and the 1951 F9F-6 Cougar was born. The much improved F9F-8 (pictured), with longer range, appeared in 1953.

Bottom left: In 1953 Vought began building the F7U-I Cutlass at a new plant at Dallas, Texas. The design was radical, having a cantilever mid-mounted trapezoid wing, swept at an angle of 38 degrees with slats along the entire span of the leading-edge (lateral control was by elevons, which handled the functions of both elevators and ailerons). The first XF7U-1, with two Westinghouse J34-WE-22 engines, flew on September 29, 1948. Only 14 F7U-Is were produced, and the planned order for 88 F7U-2s, which were to have been powered by the J34-WE-42, was cancelled. The first of the 192 F7U-3s did not reach the fleet until 1954 (with VC-3).

Bottom: Two-seat F7F-3N Tigercat USN night-fighter based in Japan during the Korean War. The F7F-3N, of which 60 were built, (plus 13 F7F-4Ns), had a longer nose housing the SCR-70 radar, but the .50 inch guns as mounted in the nose of the F7F-3 single-seat version were deleted.

The first of 792 MiGs to be destroyed in the Korean War was shot down. The F-86 was state-of-the-art, with speed brakes, all flying tailplanes, powered controls and pressurized cockpit; partial-pressure survival suits and "bonedomes" added to the glamor and technology. By mid-July 1953 the Communist offensive had spluttered to a halt. On July 22 the last combat between MiG and Sabre occurred. Five days later the Communists signed an armistice and an uneasy peace reigned once again in the Land of the Morning Calm.

Right: MiG-15 UTI "Midget". Well over 12,000 MiG-15s of all variants were built—the first flying in 1949—and the type was also built under license in China, Czechoslovakia, and Poland. The two-seat version of the MiG 15 became the standard advanced trainer in the absence of a suitable production version of the MiG-17 or MiG-19.

Home-grown & Flown
American supersonic

Left: F-105D-5 58-1173 armed with bombs. F-105 Thunderchiefs were used throughout the Vietnam War, starting with the first *Rolling Thunder* Operation on March 2, 1965. Conceived from the outset as a fighter-bomber, the Republic F-105 in the definitive single-seat "D" version, could carry up to 12,000 lb of external ordnance.

Korea proved the wrong place to deploy advanced combat aircraft. It revealed above all the need for a lightweight, uncomplicated, high performance fighter. MiGs were constantly in the air while American jets were grounded with all kinds of unserviceable equipment that pilots did not want anyway. Sabre pilots tore out every complicated piece of equipment like the APG-30 gunsight in an effort to reduce weight. Though the U.S. traditional superiority in air power eventually triumphed, the conflict had identified an urgent need for powerful new aircraft designs to replace earlier models like the Lockheed P/F-80 and even the North American F-86 Sabre, which had a most impressive kill ratio over the MiGs.

Despite their greater experience, F-86A Sabre pilots found it increasingly difficult to maintain air superiority over the Communist air force in Korea; but these early Sabres were superseded by more powerful F-86E and F-86F versions with greatly improved wing design. Lower drag from the smoother wing entry increased the F-86F top speed from 688 to 695 mph at sea level and from 604 to 608 mph at 35,000 ft, while range was slightly increased. Most importantly of all maneuverability at high altitudes and Mach numbers improved significantly. The extended-wing version made a huge difference to air fighting in Korea and F-86 Sabre pilots enjoyed an even greater superiority over the MiG-15. *(Cont. page 101)*

Right: Northrop F-5A Freedom Fighters and F-5B two-seat trainers in formation. On April 30, 1964 the first F-5Bs were delivered to the 4441st Combat Crew Training Squadron. In October 1965 12 combat ready F-5As were despatched to Vietnam with the 40503rd Tactical Fighter Wing for operational service trials under the code-name Project Skoshi Tiger ("little tiger"). It was this tour of duty which gave the aircraft its famous nickname. Eighteen F-5s operated from Bien Hoa until 1967 when they were given to the South Vietnamese Air Force.

Below: The General-Electric sponsored publicity flight on June 8, 1966, just before the No.2 North American XB-70A Valkyrie (center) was involved in a collision with F-104G/N (013) N813NA (2nd from bottom). The pilot of 013, Dr. Joseph A. Walker, and Major Carl S. Cross USAF, co-pilot of the Valkyrie, were both killed. Alvin S. White, pilot, survived.

On November 3, 1952 North American received a contract for 175 F-86H aircraft, a more powerful fighter-bomber version of the F-86F. The first of two prototypes was flown on April 30, 1953. On November 22, 1952 the first Republic F-84F Thunderstreak swept-wing fighter based on the company's earlier straight winged F-84 Thunderjet flew. As a result of experience gained in Korea, both the F-84F and the F-86H were armed with six .50-in. caliber machine-guns. However, the F-86H-5 and subsequent Sabre production batches were armed with four 20mm M-39 cannon. The F-86H was also designed to carry a 1,200-lb atomic bomb externally and release it by using a special delivery technique called "toss

Previous page: F-8E Crusader of the USN in flight.

Left: F-101As were equipped with the MA-7 fire-control system as well as with LABS (Low Altitude Bombing System) computers for toss release of their external 1,620 lb or 3,721 lb special store (nuclear bomb). The last F-101A was delivered on November 21, 1957.

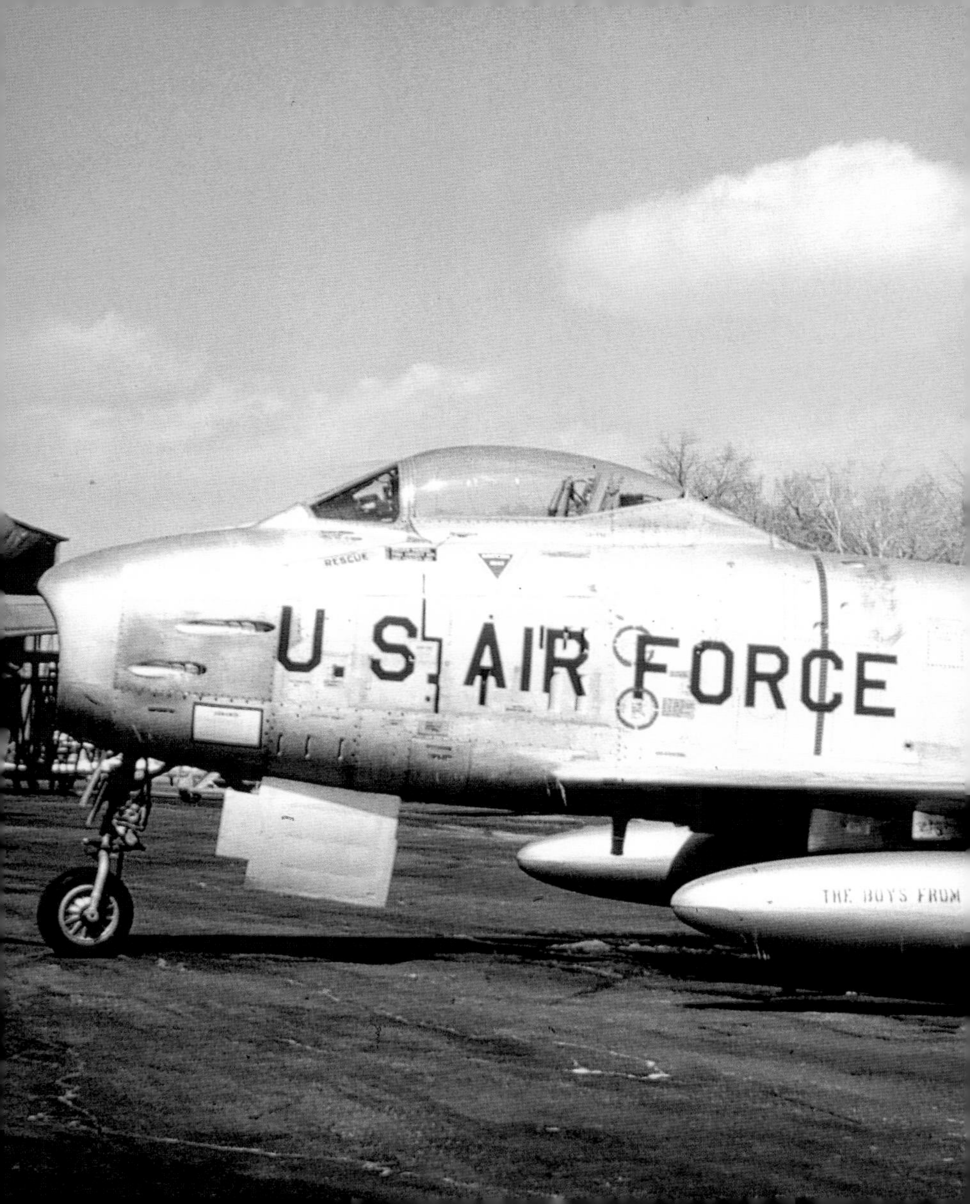
RESCUE
U.S. AIR FORCE
THE BOYS FROM

Previous page: The F-86H was the final production version of the Sabre for the USAE Four 20-mm cannon replaced the six machine-guns in the nose and it had increased span, length and a deeper fuselage. At Columbus, Ohio, 473 were produced by North American from January 1954 to August 1955. Pictured is F-86H-NH 53-1521 of the 138th Fighter Squadron, 174th Fighter Wing, NY ANG.

bombing" with the exact moment to release the bomb accurately being automatically computed by a LABS (Low Altitude Bombing System). Conventional weapons options included two 1,000-lb or smaller bombs, two 750-lb napalm bombs, or eight 5-in HVAR missiles. The last F-86H was delivered to the USAF on March 16b 1956. In December that year the 6,210th and final F-86 Sabre was accepted by the USAF.

By August 1957 some 2,711 F-84F Thunderstreaks had been built and these were used to equip six SAC escort-fighter wings and six TAC fighter-bomber wings while 1,301 examples were used to equip NATO air forces. After replacement by F-100 Super Sabres in TAC the USAF Thunderstreaks were transferred to the ANG although four F-84F TFWs were re-activated in 1961 and these served until replacement by F-4C Phantoms by July 1964. The F-86H, on the other hand, enjoyed only a relatively brief career. Four Fighter Day Wings converted to the F-100 Super Sabre in 1956-57 and the 4th FDW continued to

Right: After World War II, old piston fighters like the P-51 Mustang, F4U Corsair, and Hawker Sea Fury hit the air racing circuit at Reno, Nevada, and other venues. The FAI record for a piston-powered aircraft is 517 mph by Frank Taylor in a modified P-51D over Mojave, CA, in 1983.

Below: F-8U-1 (F-8A) of VF-211 "Fighting Checkmates."
When war broke out in Southeast Asia in 1964, F-8Es
were the first aircraft to fire their guns in anger, on
August 2. On June 12, 1966 Cdr Harold L. "Hal" Marr, CO
of VF-211, became the first Crusader pilot to shoot down
a MiG when he destroyed a MiG-17 with his second
Sidewinder missile at only 50ft.

operate the F-86H only until early 1958, when it too received F-100 aircraft. The F-86H equipped seventeen ANG units and for a short time in 1957, large numbers of F-86Hs were issued to the AFRes until it was decided to wholly re-equip the Reserve for a transport role.

Meanwhile, in April 1953, the F-86D "Sabre Dog" All-Weather fighter version which had been undergoing engineering design work since March 1949 finally entered service with active ADC units and by the end of 1953 600 F-86Ds were in service. The "D" differed radically from earlier models in having a 30-in fiberglass radome housing the antenna of the Hughes AN/APG-36/-37 search radar above a nose intake. Originally it had been envisaged that the F-86D design would be a two-seat interceptor armed solely with missiles, with the second crewmember assisting the pilot in making radar-controlled interceptions and being responsible for navigation. However, improved automated AI radar, which reduced the operator's workload, became available

Right: F-4B Phantoms of VF-84 "Jolly Rogers" and VF-41 "Black Aces" and A-4 Skyhawks of the USS *Independence* at sea.

Main picture: F-4B Phantoms of VF-41 "Black Aces" with a Vigilante and A-4 Skyhawks of VA-86 "Sidewinders" and (far right) F-4B Phantoms of VF-84 "Jolly Rogers" aboard the USS *Independence*.

Inset: The F11F-1 (F-11A) Tiger, the USN's first carrier-based supersonic fighter, was originally designated F9F-9 (for the first six aircraft) as a Cougar variant. BuNo-138604 was the first of two short-nosed flying prototypes completed in July 1954 and was used in the initial trials.

and the second crew concept was abandoned; but pilot workload was high and required more pilot training than any other type in USAF service. Some 2,504 F-86Ds were built for the USAF and by mid-1955 1,026 of Air Defense Command's 1,405 interceptors were F-86Ds, equipping twenty ADC wings. Late in 1953 some Sabre Dogs were assigned to the 5th AF in Korea but being much heavier than earlier F-86s, they had difficulty operating from the rudimentary South Korean airstrips and were soon withdrawn. After first-line service, F-86Ds were also allocated to ANG units.

The Navy had also learned lessons from air combat in Korea, which had proved that neither the Grumman F9F Panther nor the McDonnell Banshee could operate in MiG-dominated airspace without unacceptable losses; so the USN showed renewed interest in carrier-borne swept-wing fighters. One of these was the FJ-1 Fury, a North American Aircraft design proposal for a navalized version of the F-86E-10 Sabre. NAA originally received a contract to build 100 Furys for the USN but its performance was inferior to the XP-86 in all but range and only one USN fighter squadron ever operated the FJ-1. The Fury was nonetheless the first high-performance fighter to enter USN service and

Right: F-4C-19-MC 63-7566 of the USAF. The F-4C was the first Phantom to equip the USAF and was developed from the USN F-4B, which was found to outperform all USAF fighters by a wide margin. It differed from the naval version in having dual controls, an inertial navigation system, J79-GE-15 turbojets, boom-flight refuelling and provision for a large external weapons load. It also retained the folding wing and arrestor gear of the F-4B.

Right: In all, 2,474 F-84F Thunderstreak fighter-bombers were built by Republic at Long Island, and 237 were completed by General Motors-Fisher of Kansas City, Missouri. 1,301 Thunderstreaks were used by NATO air forces. In total no fewer than 7,886 F-84E/G and F-84F Thunderstreaks and RF-84F Thunderflashes were built.

Right: The F-86D "Sabre Dog" all-weather interceptor differed radically from earlier Sabres in having a 30-in fiberglass radome housing the antenna of the Hughes radar. News that the Soviet Union had detonated a nuclear device gave the program added impetus. In October 1949 NAA received a letter of intent for 122 production F-86Ds; though the first entered service as late as April 1953.

it became the first American Navy jet to operate from a
carrier in squadron strength. The Navy looked to new
designs rather than a conversion of an existing air force
design and the McDonnell FH-1 Phantom was the first
American jet aircraft to be designed for aircraft carrier
operation from the outset. In 1955 design work was begun
on the low-cost yet supersonic Northrop F-5, with added
refinements to meet a Navy specification; but by June 1956
the Navy had lost interest. (In the event only a few F-5As
equipped the USAF, although like the F-104G Starfighter,

Left: North American T-28 Trojan revealing the massive 800 hp Wright R-1300 engine. The T-28 had been built as a two-seat UAF and USN trainer from 1949-57, when T-37 jets replaced it. The French used converted T-28D Fennecs as a low-cost ground attack aircraft in Algeria. From 1961–69, North American converted over 300 T-28s to T-28Ds and in November 1961 the first examples began equipping the Vietnamese Air Force. T-38Ds were used by the 1st Air Commando Squadron against the Viet Cong until April 1964, when two U.S. pilots were killed when their T-28D wings failed.

Far right: USAF F-105D Thunderchiefs of the 34th Tactical Fighter Squadron, 388th Tactical Fighter Wing, loaded with 750 lb bombs en route to target in Southeast Asia during "Combat Sky Spot Mission," December 1968. The "Thud's" operational capability in Vietnam improved from 1966 onwards when F-4 Phantoms began to escort them on strikes.

Right: The F-4E was a multi-role fighter designed for the close-support, interdiction and air-superiority roles. Production lasted 17 years and in that time 959 were built for the USAF. Others were transferred to various air forces. Deliveries to Tactical Air Command (TAC) began in October. Pictured is F-4E 69-0268 of the 347th TFW, TAC, at Moody AFB, Georgia.

the F-5 Freedom Fighter found a ready worldwide market in NATO and with smaller friendly nations). The first swept-wing fighter to enter Navy service was the Grumman F9F-6/8 Cougar, a fighter version of the straight-winged Panther. Some 1415 F9F-6/-7 and -8 fighter versions had been built when Cougar production finally ceased in February 1960. The Navy finally went supersonic on July 30, 1954, when the F11F-l Tiger became the first supersonic operational carrier-borne naval interceptor in the world. *(Cont. page 122)*

Left: F-4Es operated by Tactical Air Command equipped the USAF Air Demonstration Squadron (4510th ADS) at Nellis AFB during a five-year period. After converting from F-100Ds, the Thunderbirds made their debut in F-4Es at the Air Force Academy in Colorado Springs, Colorado, on June 4, 1969. Rising fuel costs forced the Thunderbirds to convert to T-38A Talons in 1974.

Previous page: F-8 Crusader of VF-162, about to be launched from the port cat on the USS *Ticonderoga* in the Gulf of Tonkin, July 1969.

Right: F-4C Phantom 64-0890. During the war in Southeast Asia F-4C crews claimed the destruction of 22 MiGs with AIM Sidewinders, 14 with AIM-7 Sparrows, four with gunfire, and two by causing them to crash while maneuvering.

The Tiger had originally been designated F9F-9 (as a Cougar variant) but it was re-designated F11. The Tiger was the first aircraft to use the "Coke bottle" fuselage or "area rule" concept—a system of drag reduction—from its early stages. Deliveries of the Tiger commenced in March 1957 and production continued until December 1958. Two

first line squadrons in the Atlantic Fleet and three in the
Pacific were equipped with Tigers but the type was phased
out in 1959 and assigned to training units.

On October 6, 1954 the Chance-Vought F-8 Crusader,
the first jet fighter in the world with a variable incidence
wing, flew for the first time. It was the result of a 1952 US

Above: F-4E Phantom 74-1639 armed with a 20mm Vulcan rotary cannon and in the intercept role could carry four or six AIM-7E as well as four AIM-9D AAM missiles.

Left: USMC F-4 Phantoms of VMFA-232 refuelling from KC-130s over the Johnson Islands on a transpacific flight to Vietnam, in March 1969.

Navy requirement for a supersonic air-superiority day fighter and the Crusader beat off competition from seven other company designs to win the competition in May 1953. The prototype XF-80-1 was first flight tested on March 25, 1955. After trials the Navy accepted the F-8A in 1956. Navy fighter strength reached a peak in 1956 with 79 Navy and Marine Corps squadrons. On April 16, 1956 the Navy took delivery of the first Douglas F4D-1 Skyray short-range delta-wing interceptors after test problems had delayed the type's introduction to service with both the USN and USMC. The Skyray had a fast climb, a high ceiling speed and good radar but it was difficult to fly. Production ceased in December 1958 after

419 Skyrays had been built and the aircraft was phased out by 1964. Deliveries of the first F8U-1s to the Navy were made in March 1957. The F-8 carried internally mounted four 20mm Mk 12 cannon and early models had 32 rockets in a tray hinged to the giant belly airbrake. The Crusader remained in production for eight years and some 1,259 examples were built. In 1966–71 446 aircraft were rebuilt to a later standard. F-8D and E versions had the rockets deleted but four Sidewinders were fitted on the sides of the fuselage. In the 1960s the Crusader proved so popular with its pilots that they dubbed the aircraft "The last of the gunfighters." They also said that, "When you are out of F-8s you're out of fighters." By 1968 Crusaders had accounted for 19 MiGs destroyed from the Navy total of 34 downed in air combat in Southeast Asia; though 83 Crusaders were lost in action.

Learning the lessons of the Korean War the USAF meanwhile forged ahead with supersonic jet fighter designs. One of the first post-Korean War jet fighters was the

Right: 117. The Republic F-105 Thunderchief, or the "Thud" was designed as a successor to the F-84F and was the largest single-seat single-engined combat aircraft in history. It was unkindly reported that Republic had initially intended to make the F-105 out of concrete until they found that metal would be heavier! A total of 71 F-105Bs were issued to the 335th Tactical Fighter Squadron, 4th TFW (1958-59) for service trials. USAF F-105D Thunderchiefs had been withdrawn from Southeast Asia by October 1970, but the F-104G "Wild Weasel" (modified two-seater F-105F) equipped as an electronic warfare platform to neutralize the guidance system of the SAM missiles, stayed until the end of the Vietnam War.

Right: An F-4 refuelling from a KC-135 tanker while two other Phantoms armed with 500 lb laser guided bombs fly over during a Vietnam mission, November 1971.

McDonnell F-101A Voodoo, which was based on the company's earlier XF-88 twinjet escort fighter. Like the McDonnell F-3H Demon, the Voodoo was too late for service in the Korean War. In October 1948 the McDonnell Aircraft Company had begun testing the Voodoo but a shortage of funds had led to the cancellation of the F-101A project in 1950. However, the project was revived in 1951 to meet the need for a long-range escort fighter for Strategic Air Command's B-36 Peacemaker long range bombers and an initial contract for 39 aircraft was placed in 1952. The first F-101A flew on September 29, 1954 and deliveries of 77 F-101As and 47 F-101Cs with wings strengthened for low altitude tactical bombing were begun in 1956–57. The Voodoo was the first 1,000-mph fighter in production and the heaviest single seat fighter to serve with the USAF. By the time of its introduction the Voodoo's intended role of

Right: F-4E Phantoms 72-1479 and 72-1135 of the 335th TFS, 4th TFW, TAC based at Seymour Johnson AFB, North Carolina. This unit operated under the control of the 8th TFW at Ubon, RTAFB from July to December 1972.

fighter escort was replaced by the need for a low-altitude fighter-bomber that could deliver the Mk.7 nuclear bomb and in May 1957 they entered service with Tactical Air Command instead. The last Voodoo fighters were retired in January 1966 when they were replaced by F-4 Phantoms. Some 480 F-101B two-place long-range interceptor Voodoos were built for Air Defense Command. The first

flew on March 27, 1957 and the type equipped 17 ADC Fighter-Interceptor squadrons between January 1959 and March 1961, when Voodoo production ceased after 807 aircraft had been built.

F-101A/Cs were transferred to the ANG in 1966 and were rebuilt as RF-101G and R-101H aircraft, serving until the mid-1970s.

Left:. Among the last Grumman Cougars were 110 F9F-8P aircraft fitted with seven cameras (delivered August 1955–July 1957). These served photographic squadrons until February 1960. Here, an F9F-8P of VFP-62 shares the deck with F9F-8 BuNo141665 of VA-44, about to be catapulted off the carrier deck. F9F-8Bs were finally phased out in 1958-59, while F9-8Ps were the last Cougars to serve a fleet squadron, being retained by VFP-62 until February 1960.

Left: Grumman Cougar coming into land. The Cougar was originally a swift reaction to the arrival of the swept-wing MiG-17 in 1950. It retained the fuselage, vertical tail surfaces, power plant, and undercarriage of the straight-wing Panther.

The end of the Korean War had removed the need for a high-performance air superiority fighter from the priority list, which was bad news for the Lockheed Company who were developing the XF-104 (later called the Starfighter) for this role.

On September 11, 1950 the Lockheed XF-90 Penetration Fighter had lost out to the McDonnell XF-88A Voodoo and it seemed the company's foray into fighter design was stillborn. However, Lockheed identified a new opportunity when the project to replace the Convair F-102 Delta Dagger—the world's first supersonic, all-weather fighter-interceptor—with the F-106 Delta Dart (by 1954), was delayed. The Dart prototype flew on December 26, 1956 but F-106A interceptors did not enter service with Air Defense Command until July 1959, becoming the last single-mission fighters in Air Force service. Lockheed changed the XF-104 mission to that of air defense fighter-interceptor with a secondary role as an air superiority fighter. By the end of 1956 Lockheed had orders for 146 F-104A and six two-place F-104B aircraft for Air Defense Command and 77 single-seat F-104C fighter-bombers for Tactical Air Command. TAC looked to the Starfighter because it needed a supersonic tactical strike fighter (fighter-bomber) to replace the North American F-100C Super Sabre; the Republic F-105B Thunderchief had been delayed.

Right: Beginning on April 3, 1972 the first F-106A/Bs were delivered to the ANG when Montana's 186th FIS took delivery of its Darts. By 1974 six ANG squadrons were flying F-106s and in mid-1983 130 Darts were still operational with ANG wings. Montana relinquished its "Sixes" in 1987 in order to re-equip with F-16A/Bs. The last Darts were retired from first-line service in 1988.

Below: On May 10, 1972 Lt Randall "Randy" H. Cunningham (pilot) and Lt (jg) William P. Driscoll (RIO) of VF-96 became the first U.S. fliers to qualify as aces solely as a result of Vietnam air action when they downed their third, fourth, and fifth MiGs before their F-4J was hit by a SAM and went down off the coast. Both men ejected and were rescued by a helicopter from the USS *Okinawa* and returned uninjured to the *Constellation*.

The "Thud" was designed as a successor to the F-84F and was the largest single-seat, single engine combat aircraft in history. On its first flight on October 22, 1955 the YF-105A exceeded the speed of sound. The F-105B, which flew for the first time on May 26, 1956 was intended primarily for day operations. Only 75 F-105s were built, becoming operational with TAC in January 1959. (*Cont. page 148*)

Left: The Republic F-105D all-weather fighter-bomber version first flew on June 9, 1959 and 610 were built (1960-64). It was distinguishable from the F-105B by its bigger nose, which housed the NASARR R-14A monopulse radar for use in both high and low level missions, and Doppler navigation for night or bad weather operations. In 1971 all surviving F-104Ds were transferred to the ANG. Two F-105G squadrons served TAC's 35th TFW until 1980, when replaced by F-4Gs.

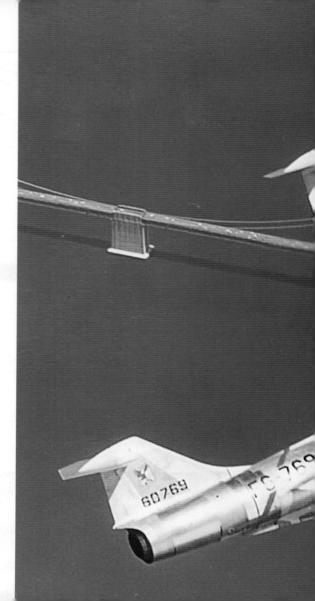

Previous page: F-4D-32-MC Phantoms of the 3rd TFW, Pacific Air Forces (PACAF) based at Clark AFB, Philippines. The bulged fairing under the nose radome contains the pre-amplifier and antennas for the APR-25/26 radar homing and warning system (RHAWS).

Right: F-104As of the 83rd Fighter Interceptor Squadron from Hamilton AFB, San Francisco, in formation.

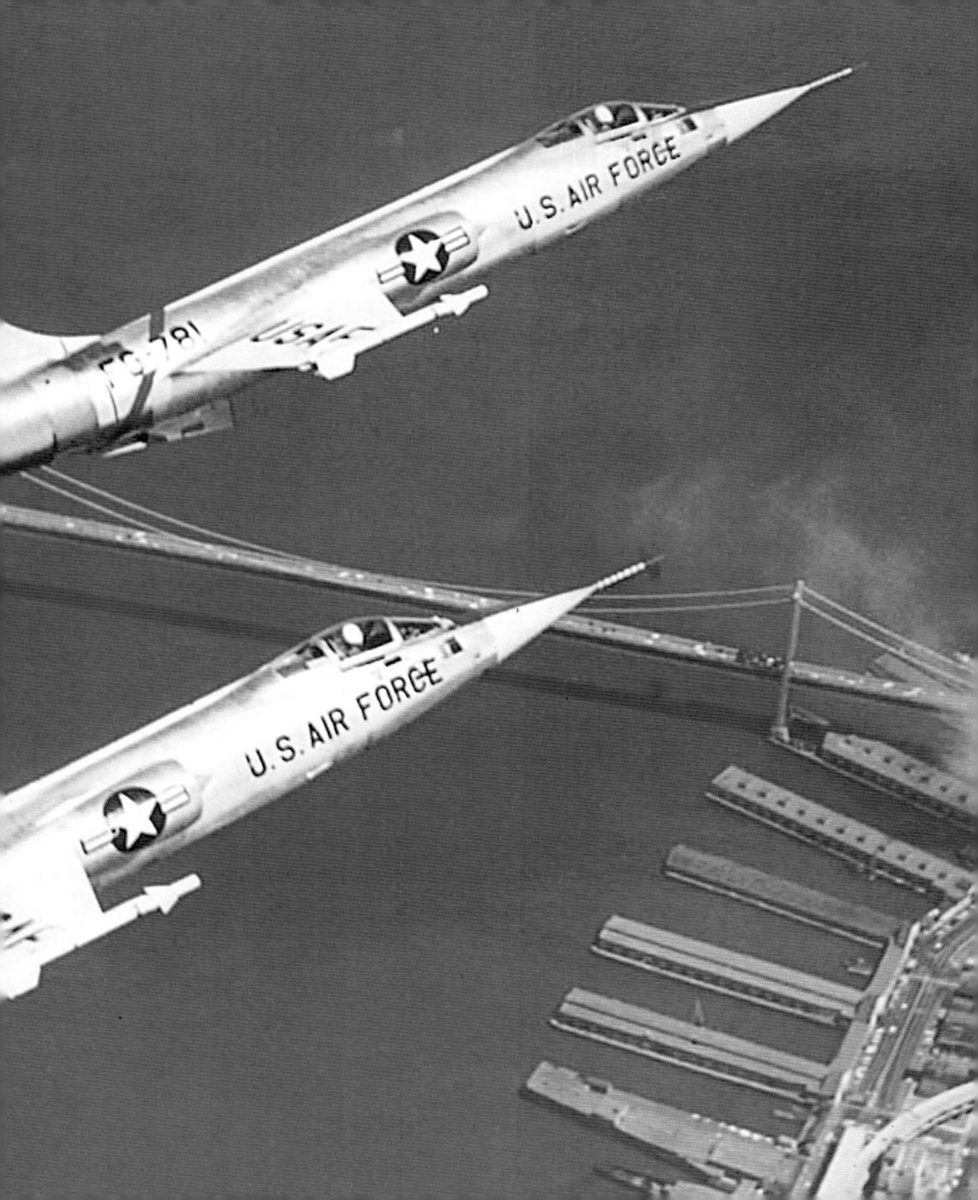
U.S. AIR FORCE
U.S. AIR FORCE

Right: F-106A Delta Dart of the 194th Fighter Interceptor Squadron, 144th Fighter Interceptor Wing, California ANG, firing a missile. The 144th FIW converted from F/TF-102A Delta Daggers in the summer of 1974 and operated Delta Darts until conversion to the F-4D in the winter of 1984.

These were followed by 600 F-105D models. The 'D, which was flown for the first time on June 9, 1959, introduced a NASARR monopulse radar for use in both high and low-level missions and doppler navigation for night or bad weather operations. By the early 1960s the F-105D had become the primary strike-fighter with TAC and USAFE. Production of the F-105 ceased in 1965 with the

two-place F-105F model but about 350 F-105Ds were
rebuilt during the Vietnam War and about thirty F-105Fs
were converted to F-105G "Wild Weasel" ECM attackers.
During 1979–80 some Thuds were transferred to the ANG
and Air Force Reserve. Typical armament consisted of four
Shrike missiles or two Standard ARMs. On January 26,
1958 the first production F-104As were issued to ADC.

Above: F-106A of the 159th Fighter Interceptor Squadron, 125th Fighter Interceptor Group, Florida ANG in 1976 bicentennial colours at Jacksonville. The Florida ABNG operated Delta Darts from July 1974 until 1987.

Left: TF-15A (F-15B-4) 71-291, a two-seat, advanced trainer in American Bicentennial colors in 1976. The first TF-15A, later redesignated F-15B, flew for the first time on July 7, 1973.

The Starfighter had the speed and the altitude to deter an aggressor, but the anticipated early availability of more flexible supersonic fighters, and the lack of an all-weather radar capability led to a review of the entire F-104 program. By December 1958 the USAF had cut back its F-104 orders to just 296 and during 1960 the F-104s were phased out of Air Defense Command (later Aerospace Defense Command). Beginning in February 1960 they were transferred to three fighter interceptor squadrons in the

Right: Super Sabre F-100D-75-NA, 56-3179. The F-100D first flew on January 24, 1956 and 1,274 examples were built. In 1962 TAC began replacing its F-100s with F-4 Phantoms but ten F-100 wings remained in service in 1964. Four TAC F-100D wings also operated on rotation in Vietnam from August 1964 to July 1971, where they were outstanding in the low-level attack and high cover roles, armed with four M-39 20 mm cannons, GAM-83A Bulldog missiles, GAR-8 sidewinder missiles, and rockets. The F-100D was not without its problems, with over 500 lost between mid-1956 and mid-1970. The last F-l00Ds were those of the 27th TFW, retired June 1972. The ANG continued to operate the "Hun" until November 10, 1979.

ANG. The "missile with the man it" had seemed destined for a bright future in the USAF.

The McDonnell F-4 Phantom, one of the most famous fighters in the history of aviation, flew for the first time (as the YF4H-1) on May 27, 1958 and in December was declared winner of the missile-armed, all-weather naval fighter competition against the Vought F8U-3 Crusader III. On July 3, 1959 the F4H-1 was named Phantom II. During 1959–1962 Phantoms set a series of new world speed and height records. The US Navy used Phantoms to replace its F9F Panther and F2H Banshee straight-winged jets, while the F-8 Crusader became the standard carrier-based fighter. Despite being designed as a specialized carrier-borne aircraft, the Phantom was to become the most widely used American supersonic fighter during the Mach.2 missile-launching fighter era. During the late 1950s the USAF had consistently refused to consider the Phantom for

Previous page: F-100D Super Sabres in formation. While the F-100A had been an air superiority fighter, the F-100C had six external ordnance stations for its enhanced fighter-bomber role. The F-100D took this operational versatility to a new level, and could carry up to 6,000 lb of external ordnance.

Above: F-100D-50-NH Super Sabre 55-2887 air refuelling with a KC-135 tanker.

Right: The F-100F combat trainer fitted with two M-39E cannon first flew on March 7, 1957 and when production ended in October 1959, 339 examples had been built. That same year 15 of the F-100Fs were modified to carry GAM-83 (later AGM-12B) Bullpup air-to-ground missiles.

interceptor service. In 1961 newly appointed Defense Secretary Robert S. McNamara sought to reduce defense expenditure by standardizing as much of Armed Forces equipment as possible. The USAF had to reconsider the Phantom, first as a potential successor to the F-106A Delta Dart interceptor in Air Defense Command and later as a multi-role tactical fighter and tactical reconnaissance aircraft in the interceptor role. The F4H-1 could carry far heavier loads than the F-106A over longer distances while having a 25 percent greater radar range. In the tactical fighter role the F4H-1F proved infinitely more versatile than the Republic F-105D Thunderchief, being able to carry external stores of conventional ordnance and having much the better all-round air superiority performance.

In April 1962 DoD announced that versions of the Phantom were to become the standard fighter and tactical reconnaissance aircraft of TAC, USAFE, and PACAF. The first F-4C flew on May 27, 1963 and in November the first production examples entered service with the USAF. They began beginning operational service with TAC units in January 1964. On August 5, 1964 the first F-4 combat sorties in the war in Southeast Asia were flown during Operation *Pierce Arrow*, when F-4Bs from the USS Constellation in the Gulf of Tonkin provided cover for retaliatory air strikes against North Vietnamese gunboats and shore facilities. On July 10, 1965 F-4 Phantoms recorded the first USAF victories of the war when they shot down two MiG-17s. On January 8, 1973 an F-4D destroyed a MiG-21, the 137th and final USAF victory of the war.

Including prototypes and development aircraft, 1,264 F-4s were delivered to the US Navy and USMC and 2,640

Phantoms to the USAF. Only the F-86 Sabre/FJ Fury exceeded the Phantom in numbers produced, but in terms of longevity, the North American design had a shorter career span than the Phantom.

North American capitalized on its F-86 Sabre design and evolved the Sabre 45 which got its name from the 45 degree angle sweptback wing. It began life as a private venture and two years were to elapse before North American were awarded a USAF contract for two YF-100 prototypes. The YF-100 flew for the first time on May 25, 1953 and on October 29 that year the F-100A set a New

Previous page: Project *High Jump* F4H-1 149449 being flown on April 3, 1962, when over NAS Point Mugu Lt Cdr John W. Young USN climbed to 25,000m (82,021 ft) in 230.44 sec.

Left: Four Grumman F11F-1s of VF-21 in echelon formation, one of the two Atlantic Fleet squadrons that flew Tigers (the other being VF-33). The Tiger also equipped five Pacific Fleet squadrons, production continuing until December 1958. The last of 201 F11F-1s produced was delivered on January 23, 1959.

World Air Speed Record of just over 755 mph on this, its maiden flight. It had become the world's first operational fighter capable of level supersonic performance and it entered production as the Super Sabre, beginning equipping the USAF in late November 1953. However, exactly one year later following a series of crashes, the "Hun," as it was known, was grounded until the wings and fin had been strengthened. Although total production only reached 2,294, the Super Sabre was still in service during the Vietnam War, proving an outstanding low-level attack and high-cover aircraft. The F-100C version, which carried more fuel than previous models and was fitted with an air-refueling probe on the right wing, pioneered global deployment of tactical aircraft by means of the probe-drogue refueling system. The first F-100C flew on January 17, 1955 and 476 examples were built. They began service entry with Tactical Air Command in July 1955.

The F-100D, which first flew on January 24, 1956, differed from the F-100C in having additional wing and tail area and an autopilot. It could carry a wide range of

Right: AIM-9J armed Northrop F-5E of the 425th Tactical Fighter Training Squadron, 405th Tactical Training Wing from Luke AFB, Arizona, in August 1979. The mission of TTL (Tactical Training Luke) was to train aircrews in fighter aircraft tactics and weapons delivery for the Tactical Air Command, USAFE, PACAF, and AAC. Tactical Training Luke also trained fighter pilots for the Air Forces of Allied nations.

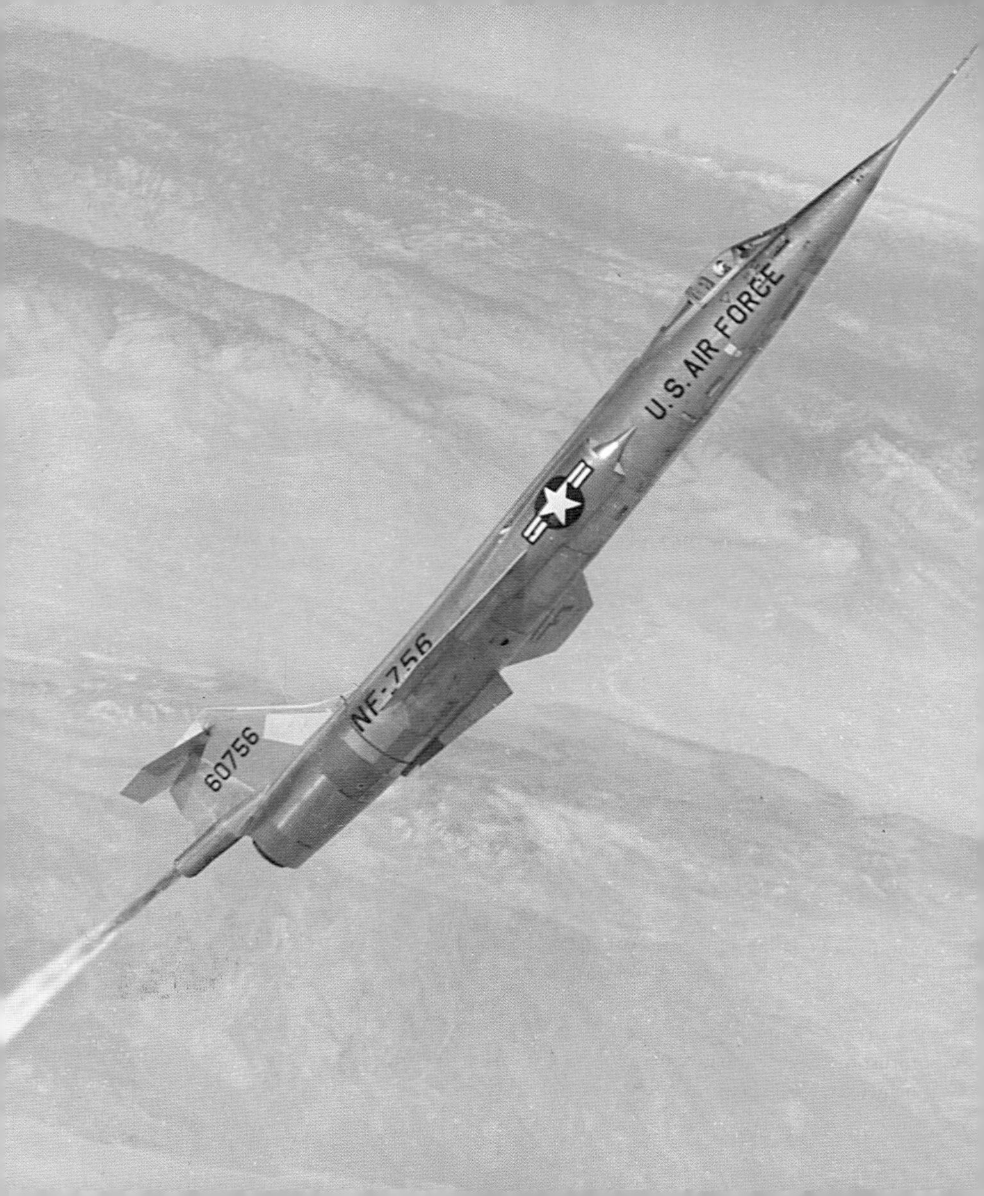
U.S. AIR FORCE
NF-756
60756

external stores options including a 1,680 lb Mk.7 nuclear bomb, as well as four GAR-8 Sidewinder air-to-air missiles. Some 1,274 F-100Ds were built by August 1959 and additionally, 339 F-100F two-seat trainers were built by October that same year. (Seven F-100Fs were later modified to "Wild Weasel" ECM versions and were used in Vietnam from December 1965).

The F-100D first entered service with Tactical Air Command in September 1956 and by June 1957 16 TAC wings were equipped with Super Sabre aircraft. As the F-100D inventory grew ever larger, from February 1958 the older F-100As and F-100Cs were gradually passed on to the ANG squadrons. In 1962 TAC began replacing its Super Sabres with F-4 Phantoms but ten wings were still equipped with Super Sabres in 1964, when sporadic fighting in Indochina erupted into full-blown conflict. Starting in August 1964, individual squadrons from four TAC wings were sent to the area on rotational tours of about six months each. Super Sabres flew more sorties than all the P-51 Mustangs in World War II. F-100Ds flew their last sorties in Vietnam in July 1971 and the last F-100Ds in USAF service were phased out in June 1972.

The Super Sabre soldiered on with ten ANG squadrons until the late 1970s and the last operational flight by an ANG F-100D took place on November 10, 1979.

In 1967 the prominence of the Soviet-built MiG-23 and MiG-25 in the air superiority role prompted the U.S. to develop the F-15 Eagle, which was expected to outperform and outclass any enemy aircraft in the foreseeable future. A low wing loading and an excellent thrust-to-weight ratio give the F-15 superb maneuverability. In addition to its primary role, the Eagle

Left: Three Starfighters were modified in 1963 to be used in the USAF astronaut training program conducted by the Aerospace Research Pilot School at Edwards AFB, California. They were fitted with a 6,000-lb thrust Rocketdyne AR-2 auxiliary rocket engine above the jetpipe, 2ft wingtip extensions and hydrogen peroxide control thrusters at the nose, tail, and wingtips.

Right: F-86H-NH 52-2017 of the 131st TFS "Polish Guard," Massachusetts ANG, at Norton AFB, California in May 1964. The Massachusetts ANG converted from F-94Cs to F-86hs in spring 1958 and operated them until March 1964, when F-84Fs began replacing the Sabres.

also has a powerful air-to-surface weapon delivery capability. Conventional stores can be carried on multiple racks below the wings without off-loading any of the air-to-air missiles.

Eighteen F-15A and two dual-seat TF-15A test and development aircraft were ordered with the first F-15A making its maiden flight on July 27, 1972. In all, 729 Eagles were ordered for the USAF with plans to equip nineteen squadrons in the U.S. and Europe where it is progressively replaced the F-4 Phantom II. The F-15C, which first flew in February 1979, differed from the F-15A in having increased fuel capacity, FAST packs on the fuselage sides and enhanced radar capability.

In the 1970s the Air Force renewed its interest in lightweight fighters once again and the USAF Lightweight Fighter Prototype program was an exercise established to evaluate and examine developments in advanced aircraft technology and design.

From among five original contenders in April 1972 the USAF finally selected two competitors, the General Dynamics YF-16 and the Northrop YF-17. The first YF-16 prototype was rolled out in December 1973 and the aircraft flew for the first time in February 1974. By mid-1974 the LWF program became more than an exercise in technological development: the winner could receive

Left: The General Dynamics (now Lockheed Martin) F-16A Fighting Falcon was born of dissatisfaction about U.S. fighter performance in Vietnam. First flown in 1974, delivery of F-16A/Bs to the USAF began in January 1979.

substantial export orders from four NATO countries wishing to replace their aging F-104G Starfighters. In late 1974 the Lightweight Fighter was being called the Air Combat Fighter (ACF). In January 1975 the USAF selected the YF-16 as its Air Combat Fighter in preference to the YF-17, primarily because of its lower production and operating costs, better range, lower aerodynamic drag, better maneuverability above Mach .8 and overall weight factor. The first of eight pre-production aircraft flew on December 8 1976 and the first full production aircraft flew on August 7 1978.

The F-16A first entered service in January 1979. The F-16C had improved radar, avionics, and increased structural strength for greater weapons load. Its initial flight was made on June 19, 1984 and deliveries to the USAF began in July that year. Over 3,000 F-16 Fighting Falcons have been delivered to Air Force fighter wings and units in the Air Force Reserve. Fourteen other nations took total production of the F-16 to 4,346 aircraft.

The F-16 is the latest in the long line of great American fighters like the F-86 Sabre, F-84F Thunderstreak, F-104 Starfighter, F-5 Freedom Fighter and the F-4 Phantom, all of which have equipped NATO countries and smaller nations of the world.

NATO WarPac

Rest of the World 1954-84

Left: In the spring of 1952 it was announced that pending the arrival of the Hawker Hunter the RAF would in the meantime receive 370 Canadair-built CL-13 Sabres, which were urgently needed to replace the ageing Vampire FB.5 and FB.9 in ten squadrons of 2nd Tactical Air Force in Germany. In November 1952 a further 60 Sabre 4s were accepted to replace the Gloster Meteor F.8s of 66 and 92 Squadrons RAF Fighter Command. Instead of deliveries by sea, to avoid the prohibitive cost of dismantling and reassembly, all the 430 Sabres were flown across the Atlantic in convoys in Operation *Becher's Brook*. Deliveries started on December 8, 1952 when the first convoy of twelve Sabres left from Quebec.

Since the 1950s Great Britain and the other European NATO countries and friendly nations around the world have traditionally operated a series of American designed and built aircraft in their air arms. British fighters had been among the world's finest in World War II. Despite post-war cuts in defense spending it gained a world lead in jet aircraft and jet engine design, producing advanced aircraft such as the Fairey Delta, the Hawker Hunter and later, the P.1A supersonic interceptor. On July 20, 1951 Neville Duke flew the Hunter prototype on its maiden flight. Two months later he was making high-speed passes in excess of 700 mph at the Farnborough Air Show.

On September 7, 1953 the Hunter broke the World Absolute Air Speed Record, which stood at 715.75 mph set by Lt Colonel William F. Barnes on July 16, 1953 in a North American F-86D Sabre, Duke achieving an average speed of 727.63 mph (Mach 0.92 at sea level). The Supermarine Swift later broke Duke's record flying at 735.70 mph. On October 6, 1954 the Fairey Delta 2 achieved supersonic status. On February 15, 1956 Peter Twiss took it through the sound barrier at its first attempt and on March 10, shattered the World Air Speed Record with a mean speed of 1,131 76 mph at 38,000 feet, exceeding the previous record by more than 300 mph. With war in Korea and rising East-West tension, however, record-breaking was an indulgence. *(Cont. Page 179)*

Above: The average airborne time for the Atlantic crossing of the Sabres from Canada (see previous page) was six hours but crossing times were dependent on the weather. The cruising altitude flown was between 30,000-35,000 ft and the intense cold at these altitudes produced aileron control locking, problems caused by the contraction of the aileron torque tubes. Landings therefore were made without using aileron.

Right: Canadair applied the designation CL-13 Sabre 2 to the license-built F-86E-6. In 1954-55, most of the RCAF's Sabre 2s were transferred under MDAP to the Greek and Turkish air arms, 104 and 105 respectively. Similarly, the Sabre 4s delivered to the RAF that were still in service in 1955-66 were reassigned under MDAP to Italy (180) and Yugoslavia (121). The F-86E Sabre was a solid and forgiving fighter, one of the few of its generation that had no glaring vice.

Right: In the mid-fifties Hawker Hunters gradually replaced the Sabres in RAF service. By June 21, 1956 some 267 Sabres had been flown back to Britain prior to transfer to USAF control. In England meanwhile, 66 and 92 Squadrons used the Sabre until spring 1956 when they re-equipped with Hunter F.4s. Between 1956 and 1958 302 Sabres were returned to USAF charge.

Above: CF-101B Voodoos of the Royal Canadian Air Force. Between July 1961 and May 1962, the RCAF received 56 F-1201Bs and ten F-101F two-seat combat-capable trainers from the USAF for the defense of North America. The Voodoos in Canadian service were redesignated CF-101Bs/CF-101Fs respectively, and they were assigned RCAF serials using the last three digits of their USAF serials.

Left: Canadian aircrews running to their CF-101Bs.

The immediate replacement of the RAF's aging de Havilland Vampire FB.5s in 2nd Tactical Air Force in Germany and Gloster Meteor fighters at home was more urgent. Indigenous designs like the P.1A (later Lightning) were still under development while the Hunter F.1 and the delta-winged Gloster Javelin two-seat all-weather fighter were experiencing delays. The Hunter F.1 would not enter service until late July 1954. (Cont. page 184)

Previous page: The Gloster Javelin appeared in eight different marks of fighter (FAW1-9) from 1954 to 1968, with production totalling 428, including 22 T.3 trainer versions. Its delta wing plan form and high tail earned it the nickname "The flying flat iron." Pictured are FAW.4s, the first version to embody an all-moving tailplane and first issued at the start of 1957. The last of RAF Fighter Command's Javelin squadrons were converted to Lightnings in October 1964.

Right: The Avro Canada CF-100 Canuck two-seat long-range all-weather fighter entered service with the RCAF in October 1951. Early versions were armed with eight machine guns in a ventral pack and later models had two wingtip pods, each with 29 70mm unguided rockets.

Though the first production Javelin flew on July 22, 1954, protracted development ensured that the first F(AW)Is were not issued to squadrons until February 29, 1956. To fill the generation gap, on November 1, 1951 three squadrons of Sabres of No 1 Fighter Wing RCAF (NATO) formed in England. Their mission, together with the F-86A Sabres of the 81st Fighter Wing USAF based in Suffolk, was the air defense of Great Britain. No.1 Fighter Wing remained in England for the next three years, at which time the UK air defense was finally undertaken by the Sabres and Hunters of RAF Fighter Command.

Early in 1949, the Canadian Government had selected the F-86A Sabre to form the nucleus of a new RCAF jet fighter force and Canadair Ltd was selected to build 350

Left: At the end of 1949 Republic began developing a swept-wing version of the F-84 Thunderjet, which was successfully achieved by using 60 percent of the latter's tooling and a standard F-84E fuselage. The production F-84F Thunderstreak first flew on 22 November 1952 and deliveries to TAC and SAC began in January 1954, with the 506th Strategic Fighter Wing being the first to receive the aircraft. Pictured is F-84F- of the Belgian Air Force.

CL-13/Sabre Mk.2s under license. In February 1952 America purchased 60 Sabre 2s from Canadair and after modification they were delivered to the USAF in April–July to equip two fighter wings in Korea. In Europe, the RCAF Sabre 2 was the only swept-wing fighter in NATO. Some 438 CL-13 Sabre Mk.4s were built but almost all of these were transferred to the RAF under the MDAP. They equipped 11 squadrons, the vast majority in West Germany, remaining in RAF service until replaced by the Hawker Hunter by June 1956. All 1,815 CL-13 Sabres were armed with six 0.50-inch M-3 machine-guns and except for the Mk 5 and Mk.6 versions, which had the Avro Orenda turbojet, were powered by J47-GE- engines. Some 647 CL-13B Sabre Mk.6s were built, of which 390 examples served in nine RCAF squadrons in Germany. In July 1959 the Canadair-built CF-104 Starfighter was selected to replace the Sabre in RCAF service, the last in Europe being retired in November 1963.

Canada had also developed the two-seat long-range all-weather CF-100 Canuck. The type first flew on January 19, 1950, powered by two Rolls-Royce Avon turbojets. When the Orenda-powered CF-100 Mk.2 flew on June 20, 1951 it was the first jet aircraft completely designed and built in Canada. Service deliveries began in October 1951 and these were followed later by the CF-100.Mk.4 and Mk.5, armed with wingtip pods containing 70 mm unguided rockets. The last Canucks were finally withdrawn from service late in 1981. Meanwhile, beginning in July 1961, the RCAF received ex-US Air Defense Command McDonnell F-101B Voodoo two-seat all weather long-range interceptors and a few F-101F two-seat combat-capable trainers from the USAF for the defense of North

Main picture: Fiat G.91R. The G91 single-seat tactical attack and reconnaissance fighter was developed early in 1954 to meet a NATO requirement but in the event only the *Aeronautica Militare Italiana* (AMI), Italian Air Force and Luftwaffe adopted the fighter for its forces. Starting in May 1962, the Luftwaffe received almost 400 examples of the G.91R/3 "Gina" for the light attack and weapons training role, with over 200 of these produced under license in Germany.

Inset: Fiat (later *Aeritalia SpA*) G.91Y of *8° Stormo* of the Italian Air Force. The G.91Y, unlike the Fiat G91R, was designed to meet an Italian Air Force requirement of 1965. The G91Y prototype first flew on December 27, 1966; 67 examples were built.

America. In 1962 the surviving CF-101Bs and CF-101Fs, as they were known in Canadian service, were exchanged for a number of refurbished aircraft from U.S. stocks. The last Canadian Voodoo was not retired until 1987.

In Britain's Royal Navy the Supermarine Attacker F.1 was the Fleet Air Arm's first jet fighter. The prototype flew in June 1947 and the first Attackers entered service in August 1951. Some 61 Attacker F.1 and FB.1s and 84 FB.2s were produced, the last being delivered in 1953. From 1954 the Supermarine Sea Hawk and De Havilland Sea Venom replaced Attackers in first-line service, although they continued to operate with the Royal Naval Volunteer Reserve (RNVR) until early in 1957. Although the Supermarine Attacker was the Royal Navy's first jet fighter to go to sea, the Hawker Sea Hawk became the standard fighter of the Fleet Air Arm. The first squadron formed in March 1953. Production of the Sea Hawk ended with the FGA.6 in 1956. After winning a contract from the Netherlands for Sea Hawks, in February 1957 the company received an order from West Germany for 68 Mk 100 and Mk 101 versions for the recently created *Bundesmarine*. These aircraft, which were powered by a 5,400-lb thrust Rolls-Royce Nene turbojet, met a requirement for a new strike and long-range reconnaissance shipboard fighter for the *Marineflieger*. Although this service had no aircraft carriers, the ability to operate from other NATO countries' carriers was desired. Though the German Sea Hawks were land-based, they retained their RN folding wings. *(Cont. page 194)*

Right: Dassault Mirage IIIC of 2nd *Escadron de Chasse* of the French Armée de l'Air at Coltishall on April 17, 1967.

Left: In 1955 the *Fuerza Aerea Venezolanas* (FAV or Venezuelan Air Force) asked the U.S. for Sabres to replace its obsolete de Havilland Vampire fighters. By 1957 Venezuela had received 22 MDAP-funded F-86Fs and these were operated by *Escuadrón de Caza 36 "Jaguares"* of *Grupo Aerea de Caza 12* at Mariscal Sucre. In the mid-1960s the Venezuelan Government placed orders with the West German Government for 78 ex-Luftwaffe F-86K Sabres. The Dassault Mirage IIIV finally replaced the last of the F-86Ks in 1971.

The Sea Hawk was retired from FAA service on December
15, 1960.

On January 19, 1956 the Supermarine Scimitar F.Mk.1
single-seat carrier-borne multi-role aircraft flew for the first
time; deliveries to the Fleet Air Arm began in June 1958.

The Scimitar was the FAA's first swept-wing single-seat
fighter and the first one capable of low-level attacks at
supersonic speeds with tactical nuclear weapons. The
aircraft also operated in the high-level interception role
with Sidewinder infrared homing air-to-air guided missiles.

Inset: Dassault Mystère IVs of the French Armée de l'Air. The Mystère IV prototype first flew on September 28, 1952 and a U.S. funded order for 225 aircraft for the Armée de l'Air was placed in April 1953.

Left: Eventual Dassault Mystère production reached 421, including 110 for India and 60 for Israel; and all were completed by October 1958. Mystère IVAs were used by the French Air force in the Suez campaign in 1956 and by India against Pakistan in the war of 1965. Israeli Mystères took part in the Six-Day War against its Arab neighbors in 1967.

Alternatively, a pod containing twelve 2-in unguided rockets could be carried. A total of 76 Scimitars was built and they equipped four first-line FAA squadrons, the last being embarked aboard the new aircraft carrier HMS Hermes in July 1960.

Plans for a supersonic Hunter using an afterburning Avon engine and 50-degree swept wing, were finally killed off in July 1953 with the cancellation of the prototype, with the ending of the Korean War. *(Cont. page 207)*

Left: The distinctive double-delta winged Saab Draken J35 equipped the Swedish *Flygvapen* from 1960 until 1998 and the type was exported to Denmark, Finland, and Austria. The double-delta arose from the desire for the greatest possible volume from a small airframe: the sharply swept inner delta provided sufficient depth to accommodate all fuel and the main undercarriage members.

Left: A Danish Air Force F-35, one of 46 Draken fighter-bomber, reconnaissance-fighter and trainer versions ordered during 1968–69. Denmark's Drakens were extensively upgraded during the mid-1980s and the last was retired in December 1993.

Below: The Rolls-Royce Nene powered Supermarine Attacker F.1 was the Fleet Air Arm's first jet fighter. It entered service with No.800 Squadron in August 1951.

Left: The Royal Norwegian Air Force was one of four NATO countries outside the U.S. to operate the Northrop F-5A. To reduce costs, fire-control radar was not fitted, a simple optical sight was used in conjunction with an Emerson ranging radar set installed in the tip of the nose.

Following page: Although the Supermarine Attacker was the Royal Navy's first jet fighter to go to sea, it was the Hawker Sea Hawk which became the standard fighter of the Fleet Air Arm. The first squadron, No.806 formed in March 1953 and carried the "Ace of Diamonds" as its motif.

Left: In the air defense role, the 24 FG.1 (F-4K) Phantoms for the RAF were assigned to No. 43 Squadron, the "Fighting Cocks" (pictured shadowing a Russian Bear over the North Sea) at Leuchars, Scotland, in September 1968, and to No. 111 "Treble One" Squadron. No.43 Squadron added the FGR.2 version in May 1988 and converted to the Panavia Tornado F.3 in 1989. Strike Phantoms were gradually switched to the air defense interceptor role.

Hawkers built 365 Hunter F.4s, which differed greatly from the F.1 and F.2, having more powerful engines, additional fuel capacity, provision for underwing stores, and a "full flying tail." The first flew on October 20, 1954. In 2nd Tactical Air Force the Hunter F.4 replaced all 10 squadrons of Sabre F.1/F.4s in five wings and the DH Venom FB.1 in squadron service. The Hunter F.6 became a highly successful fighter-ground attack

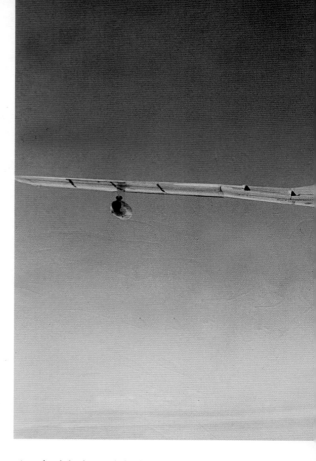

Right: A Lightning F.3 of No. 29 Squadron RAF refuelling from a Victor tanker. No.29 Squadron operated the F.3 at Wattisham, England, from May 1967 to December 1974, when it reformed as a Phantom FGR.2 Squadron at RAF Coningsby.

aircraft while the English Electric P.1 was developed (as the Lightning) to properly fulfil the role of the RAF's first true supersonic front line interceptor. In 1957 Duncan Sandys' infamous Defence White Paper predicted that the ICBM would shortly render manned interceptor aircraft obsolete and all of the Venom squadrons and nine of the thirteen

Hunter F.4 squadrons in 2nd TAF were disbanded almost immediately. The other squadrons soon followed. Hunter F.6s were replaced by the Lightning F.1A and by April 1961 only five Hunter squadrons in Fighter Command remained. The last of these re-equipped with the Lightning F.2 in early 1963. The Hunter was one of Britain's most

Left:. Lightnings of No 74 "Tiger" Squadron RAF carrying out an in-flight refuelling with a Victor tanker while en route from Tengah, Malaya, to Cyprus in 1971. No. 74 Squadron disbanded at Tengah on August 25, 1971. From September 2, 1971 all remaining Lightnings were flown on the 6,000-mile, 13-hour trip to Akrotiri, Cyprus, for transfer to 56 Squadron. they staged through Gan and Muharraq, completing seven in-flight refuellings with Victor tankers.

Following page:
Production of the Hawker Sea Hawk ended with the FGA.6 in 1956. After winning a contract from the Netherlands for Sea Hawks, in February 1957 the company received an order from West Germany for 68 Mk 100 and Mk 101 versions for the recently created *Bundesmarine*.

successful post-war designs with production totalling 1,985 examples, including 445 built in Belgium and the Netherlands, while 429 were exported as new aircraft. In excess of 700 Hunters were refurbished or completely remanufactured for more than 17 air forces.

In the early 1960s ADC and TAC dropped the F-104 from its inventories and the Starfighter story seemed to be over; but Federal Germany signed a contract for 96 F-104F/Gs and one by one other European nations followed the German lead. Nations stood in line to buy great numbers manufacturerd in seven countries, including

Germany, Belgium, Italy and Holland. The aircraft is remembered chiefly for its heavy loss rate in NATO service. Germany alone lost 281 Starfighters. The Luftwaffe needed Starfighters to replace the F-84F Thunderstreak in the strike role, the F-86 Sabre in the air defence role, and the RF-84F Thunderflash in photo-reconnaissance while the F-104 became standard equipment in the *Marineflieger*. In July 1959 Canada announced that the Canadair-built CF-104 had been selected to replace the Sabre Mk.6 and the CF-100 Canuck in the eight RCAF squadrons based in France and

Left: One of 128 license-built F-4EJs by Mitsubishi Heavy Industries at Nagoya for the *Nihon Koku Jiei Tai* (Japanese Air Self-Defense Force, or JASDF), first assigned to squadrons in August 1972.

Left: One of the 14 McDonnell-built RF-4EJ (KAI) aircraft assigned to the 501 *Hiko-tai* (squadron) of the *Teisatsu Koku-tai* (Tactical Reconnaissance Group) at Hyakuri in November 1974–June 1975. The RF-4E was an export version of the Phantom ordered by West Germany, Greece (8), Iran (10), Israel (12), Japan (14 RF-4EJ) and Turkey (8), under the Peace Trout program. It combined the photographic and multi-sensor reconnaissance system and modified nose of the RF-4C and much of the airframe of the F-4E.

Above: Though the German Sea Hawks were land-based, they retained the folding wings of the Royal Navy's FAA Sea Hawks. The Sea Hawk retired from FAA service after No. 806 Squadron returned from the Far East in 1960.

Germany. After the Canadian government's rejection of the nuclear role in 1968, CF-104s were assigned to conventional ground attack and in 1974 the M-61 cannon was installed. Beginning in 1983, any remaining CF-104s were replaced with the McDonnell Douglas CF-18 Hornet. The last CF-104s were phased out of service on March 1, 1986.

Greece operated 159 Starfighters, the last being retired in spring 1993. In Italy the F-104G became operational in March 1963. Beginning in February the much-improved F-104S all-weather interceptor version was introduced and during 1983-1993 147 F-104S models were modified to F-104S ASA or "updated weapon system" standard. In

March 1979 the last F-104, the 246th and final Italy-produced F-104S, was rolled out, bringing worldwide Starfighter production to 2,578. The introduction of the Tornado into the AMI inventory saw the gradual decline of Starfighter units and by early 2000 the Italian Starfighter inventory had been reduced to five units pending eventual replacement by the Eurofighter. The Netherlands received 156 Starfighters, the first being delivered in December 1962, where they replaced the Hawker Hunter and F-86K Sabre. From April 1979 squadrons began re-training to fly the European-built General Dynamics F-16A/B, the last squadron becoming fully operational on the Fighting Falcon on April 1, 1982. The Royal Norwegian Air Force operated Starfighters from 1963 until winter 1982–83, when F-16A/B aircraft replaced the last F-104s. Turkey operated in excess of 400 Starfighters—the majority of them second-hand from other NATO countries—from 1965 until the mid-90s. By 1986 Starfighters equipped thirteen Turkish squadrons in the close support and air defense roles. From 1993 to 1994 the General Dynamics F-16 Fighting Falcon replaced the remaining Starfighters. Japan, Pakistan (using them in the war with India in 1965 and in 1971), Spain, and Taiwan also operated Starfighters in large numbers.

In France meanwhile, Avions Marcel Dassault developed the Super Mystère (Mystery) single-seat interceptor, which first flew on February 23, 1951 and the Etendard single-seat carrier-borne fighter. The Mystère was ordered into production as the IIC and delivered to the Armee de l'Air (French air force) during October 1954–January 1957. It had a comparatively short career because of the introduction of the more advanced Mystère

IV series. The Mystère IV prototype first flew on September 28, 1952 and an American-funded order for 225 aircraft for the Armée de l'Air was placed in April 1953. Eventual Mystère IV production reached 421, including 110 for India and 60 for Israel. Mystère IVAs were used by the Armée de l'Air in the Suez campaign in 1956 and by India against Pakistan in the war of 1965. *Heyl Ha' Avir* (Israel Defense Force/Air Force) Mystères took part in the Six-Day War against Irael's Arab neighbors in 1967, but the Etendard served only with the Aéronavale (French Navy). Originally, Dassault intended to compete in the NATO contest for a lightweight interceptor but withdrew and completed the Etendard as a private venture. The aircraft made its first flight on July 23, 1956. Dassault's design was improved in the late 1960s when the Aéronavale, in preference to other designs, chose the Dassault-Bréguet Super Etendard. Dassault's Super Mystère B2 first flew on February 26, 1957 and became the first European aircraft with a Mach 1+ performance to enter full-scale service.

The other famous name in the remarkable list of Dassault-Bréguet aircraft is the Mirage series of interceptors, which serve with air forces throughout the world. The Mirage I first flew on June 25, 1955 and on October 24, 1958 a Mirage IIIA became the first West European aircraft to achieve Mach 2 in level flight. By 1977 about 1500 Mirage IIIs had been purchased by 13 countries plus the Armée de l'Air. In 1965 Israel requested a special VFR (clear weather) ground attack version of the Mirage III for Middle East operations. Designated the Mirage V, it entered production for the Armee de L'Air and eleven other nations. In the Middle East in June 1967 in

the Six-Day War between Israel and Egypt, Jordan and Syria, a preliminary Israeli air strike by Mirage IIICJs, Super Mystères and other aircraft on June 5 destroyed 300 Egyptian aircraft. The Syrian and Jordanian air forces were destroyed in 25 minutes. By June 10, 418 Arab aircraft had been destroyed for the loss of 27 Israeli aircraft.

Other members of the versatile Mirage family include the Mirage F1 single-seat multipurpose fighter which first flew on December 23, 1966. The Dassault Mirage F1C single-seat multi-mission fighter, successor to the Mirage III and Mirage 5, first flew on December 23, 1966, and first entered service with the Armée de l'Air in May 1973 when the 30th Wing at Reims began receiving its aircraft. In 1976 the F.1C's twin 30mm cannon armament was

Right: Canadian F-104G Starfighter in "Tiger" scheme in February 1972. Despite its fundamtental unsuitability for tactical strike, the Starfighter became the subject of a huge multinational manufacturing program in its F-104G guise, being built in Europe, Canada, and Japan.

supplemented by two wing-tip-mounted R530 medium-range AAM and in 1977 by two R550 Magic AAM. The French air force acquired 83 Mirage F1Cs, 20 F1B two-seaters, and 79 F1C-200 sub-variants with a fixed in-flight

refuelling probe. The F.1 series of warplanes has been exported to Morocco, Jordan, Greece, Kuwait, Ecuador, Libya, Spain, and Qatar, and was license-built in South Africa where it operated as the F1CZ. *(Cont. page 232)*

Left: CL-13B Sabre 6 23707 of 434 Squadron, 3 Fighter Wing RCAF, which was based at Zweibrücken, Germany March 1953–1963.

Right: In the beautiful blue. Hawker Hunter F.6 XG228/C of No. 92 Squadron en route to Malta in 1960. This Hunter was flown for the first time on October 2, 1956 by Neville Duke before service delivery on the 25th of the same month. Converted to FGA.9 in 1965, XG228 joined the TWU at Brawdy, Scotland, in October 1976, moving to Lossiemouth with No. 2 TWU in 1978.

FLT.LT. T.J.NELS...
C.T.RYE

DANGER
KEEP CLEAR OF INTAKE
WHEN ENGINE IS RUNNING

KEEP CLEAR WHEN
ENGINE IS RUNNING

Previous page: English Electric Lightning F.1s of 74 "Tiger" Squadron at RAF Coltishall in 1961. On November 25, 1958 the English Electric P.1B prototype became the first British aircraft to fly at Mach 2. No.74 Squadron was the first operational squadron in RAF Fighter Command to be equipped with the Lightning, in February 1960.

Above: Dassault Mirage F1C single-seat multi-mission fighter, successor to the Mirage III and Mirage 5, first entered service with the Armée de l'Air in May 1973 with the 30th wing at Reims. In 1976 the F.1C's twin 30mm cannon armament was supplemented by two wing tip mounted R530 medium-range AAM and in 1977 by two R550 Magic AAM.

Right: Squadron Leader Brian Mercer AFC* OC, No. 92 Squadron of the *Blue Diamonds* display team in his vintage Alfa Romeo in front of his Hunter F.6 XG225/M at Middleton St. George, England, in 1961.

Just as the Dassault Bréguet name is synonymous with French aviation, so too is Aeritalia (formed by Fiat's merger with Aerfer) with Italian aviation. Its most famous aircraft is probably the G.91, which was declared winner of a 1954 contest to find a standard light tactical NATO fighter. Built jointly by Italy and West Germany, then only

Right: 187. On June 13, 1974, following the withdrawal of U.S. aid and Greek secession from NATO, Greece signed an order with France for the purchase of 40 Matra 550 Magic-armed Dassault Mirage F.1CG interceptors to replace its F-102A Delta Daggers in the *Elliniki Aeropo'ria,* or Hellenic Air Force. On August 5, 1975 the first of these began to reach the 114 *Ptérix Mahis* (combat wing) at Tanagra. The last Mirage F.1CGs were delivered in 1977.

two NATO nations to use it, the G.91 was also purchased by Angola, Greece, Portugal, and Turkey.

In October 1964 the last of RAF Fighter Command's Javelin squadrons converted to the English Electric (later British Aircraft Corporation) Lightning single seat, all-weather supersonic interceptor. The P.1A (Lightning) flew

for the first time on August 4, 1954. Seven days later it broke the sound barrier, thus becoming the first RAF single-seat fighter capable of exceeding the speed of sound in level flight. On November 25, 1958 the Avon-powered Lightning P.1B became the first British aircraft ever to fly at Mach 2. The first production Lightning F.l flew for the first time in October 1959 and the type entered squadron service in July 1960, becoming the principal air defense fighter in both Fighter (later Strike) Command and RAF Germany. In 1963 the F2, with fully variable afterburner, equipped two Squadrons of RAF Fighter Command. Between 1964 and 1968 the major Lightning variant was the F3, which differed principally from earlier marks in

Below: *Turk Hava Kuvvetleri* (THK, Turkish Air Force) F-84s and RAF Hawker Hunters of the *Blue Diamonds* aerobatic display team at Diyarbakir, Turkey, same year.

having its two Aden nose cannon deleted and a pair of Red Top missiles in place of the earlier Firestreaks. In 1965 BAC developed a kinked and cambered wing to improve operation at vastly increased weights, reduce subsonic drag, and thus extend the range. This fully developed version of the Lightning was finally designated the F Mk 6. Fuel capacity was almost doubled by the installation of an enlarged ventral fuel tank containing 740 U.S. gallons. The F6 prototype first flew on April 17, 1964 and entered squadron service in November 1965. All Home Defence F3s were subsequently retrofitted to F6 standard and equipped five squadrons in Fighter (later Strike) Command.

Right: In Canada the introduction of the CF-104 Starfighter marked a change of role from air defense to nuclear strike. Operating in the strike role, the CF-104 carried a single high-yield tactical nuclear weapon on the center-line. This weapon could have been delivered using a LABS toss maneuver, or in a low-level laydown attack. In Europe CF-104s equipped eight squadrons of No.1 Air Division, beginning in December 1962. After the Canadian government's rejection of the nuclear role in 1968, CF-104s were assigned to conventional ground attack and in 1974 the M-61 cannon was installed.

By mid-1967 all Lightnings were capable of being refuelled in flight. In August that year the final Lightning was completed. From 1974 Lightnings began to be replaced by Phantoms in the air defense role and the Tornado F Mk 2 replaced the last two remaining squadrons in May 1988. In all 338 Lightnings were built, including 57 multi-role fighter and attack variants for Kuwait and the Royal Saudi Air Force.

Another historically significant aircraft, which appeared in the 1960s, was the Hawker P1127 Kestrel, the

world's first operational fixed-wing vertical/short take-off or landing (VTOL) aircraft and forerunner of the world famous Harrier "jump jet." On October 21, 1960 the P1127 made its first tethered hovering flight using a vectored-thrust turbofan and in September 1961 it made the first transition from vertical to horizontal flight. A lengthy period of development, trials, and evaluation followed and the first of six development Harriers flew on August 31, 1966. The first true production aircraft flew on December 28, 1967. Total deliveries to the RAF amounted

to 120 single-seat aircraft and 23 two-seat aircraft before the USMC took an interest and also ordered 102 AV-8A single-seaters. The Royal Navy decided to adopt the Sea Harrier version in May 1975 and the first example flew on August 20, 1978.

Meanwhile, in September 1964 Britain became the first F-4 Phantom export customer with an order for F-4K (FG Mk.Is) for the Royal Navy, followed in February 1965 by an order for 116 Spey-engined F-4M (FGR Mk.2s) for the RAF. Phantoms first entered service with the Royal Navy in April 1968 and in August the first FGR.2s entered service with the RAF. Other nations that have operated the Phantom are Egypt, Greece, Turkey, South Korea, Spain, Iran, and Japan. On November 1, 1968 two F-4EJs for Japan were ordered and the next 11 aircraft were delivered by McDonnell as knockdown kits and assembled in Japan by Mitsubishi, who then built 127 F-4EJs under license. In January 1969 the Federal German Republic ordered 88 RF-4Es for the Luftwaffe.

In September 1969 delivery of 240 F-4Es to the Tsvah Haganah le Israel—Heyl ha'Avir (Israel Defense Force/Air Force) began. During the War of Attrition in October 1969

Right: F-104G 683-400 (MM6501), the first Military Assistance Program (MAP) F-104G built by Lockheed and which was in competition on August 10, 1962 with a Fiat G91 T/3 of the Luftwaffe and G.91R of the *Aeronautica Militate Italiana* (AMI), Italian Air Force. This Starfighter served as the pattern aircraft for Fiat of Italy. The Starfighter's darkened intake lips are heating elements unique to MAP variants of the F-104G.

Above: When France stopped deliveries of the Mirage 5 to Israel, Israel Aircraft Industries Ltd produced the Nesher (Eagle) a copy of the Mirage 5. IAI took the Nesher a stage further and developed the Kfir (Lion Cub) single-seat fighter, unveiled in 1975. The improved 1977 Kfir-C2 incorporated a close-coupled canard configuration similar to the Viggen to improve combat maneuverability.

Left: The Mikoyan/ Gurevich MiG-21 single-seat multi-role tactical fighter first flew in 1955 and delivery to Soviet forces began in 1958. In February 1972 a new, cleaned-up and refined version, the MiG-21bis "Fishbed L" entered service. The MiG-21 was built in China by Chengdu as the J-7 and F-7 (for export). Pictured is a MiG-21F of the Finnish Air Force, which received the MiG-21F in April 1963.

Left: F-4F of fighter wing 71, Richthofen. By 1971 changes in the MRCA-75 (Panavia Tornado) program resulted in West Germany ordering 175 F-4Fs as part of the *Peace Rhine* program to replace the F-104G Starfighter in two *Jagdgeschwader* (JG or fighter wings) and two *Jagdbombergeschwader* (fighter-bomber wings).

Israeli F-4Es went into action during strikes against Egyptian SAM batteries. On November 11 the first Israeli F-4E air-to-air victory occurred. Some 140 Israeli F-4Es performed almost all the long-range strike missions, losing 33 in combat, mainly to ground fire, and in operational accidents. In October 1973 the Heyl ha'Avir had 432 aircraft in its inventory, of which Phantom aircraft were

Previous page: The *Aeronautica Militare Italiana* (AMI) received 124 FIAT-built F-104Gs and 24 TF-104Gs. Beginning in February 1970 the much-improved F-104S all-weather interceptor version began equipping the AMI. During 1983–1993 147 were modified to F-104S ASA (*Aggiornamiento Sistema d'Arma*) or "updated weapon system" standard. The introduction of the Tornado saw the gradual decline of Starfighter units. F-16s have been leased to the AMI pending Eurofighter.

Right: The 1975 MiG-31 "Foxhound-A" two-seat long-range interceptor. Mikoyan's design has an N-007 Zaslon radar, code-named "Flash Dance" by NATO, which uses a unique fixed phase-array antenna that points its beam electronically.

the second most numerous aircraft, against 600 aircraft operated by Egypt and 210 by Syria. Egypt and Syria invaded Israel on October 6, 1973, which was Yom Kippur, the Jewish day of atonement. Israel admitted to total losses of 115 aircraft, 60 of them in the first week of

the war. Eventually the IAF gained the upper hand on the Sinai Front by making massed attacks using squadrons of attacking aircraft, rather than in groups of four, and ground targets were bombed accurately by American-supplied "smart" bombs. Israeli Mirages were employed

Left: Yakovlev Yak-38
"Forger A" single seat
VTOL naval attack aircraft
of the Soviet Union
*Aviatsiya Voenno-
morskovo Flota* (AV-MF or
naval air force), which
made its appearance in
the early seventies.
Production had reached
about 70 aircraft by 1986.

primarily as interceptor and cover aircraft for the attacking bombers and proved to be superior to all MiG-21, Mirage III, and V aircraft flown by the Arab air forces. By the end of the war, of a total of 222 Arab aircraft downed, 162 were shot down in air combat, against five IAF aircraft. An armistice was agreed on October 24, 1973, though hostilities continued for some months.

Sweden too has produced some remarkable aircraft; not last of which is the Saab J35 Draken, which first flew on October 25, 1955. Swedish military thinking dictates that her air force must not be restricted to conventional air

Left: Unlike the Harrier, Forger had a large turbojet that exhausts through two vectoring nozzles on the rear fuselage and two much lower powered "liftjets" in the fuselage aft of the cockpit to exhaust downward and thereby contribute to the lift thrust and pitch and trim.

Previous page: Harrier GR.3 of No.1 Squadron, RAF Wittering, operating from Bardufoss, north Norway, during Exercise "Cold Winter" in March 1979.

bases but be able to operate from small, improvised airfields and main highways if necessary. This requirement led to the unique double-delta configuration, which enables the Draken to take off within only 4,000 feet. Altogether, 606 Drakens were built. The type equipped the *Flygvapen* (Royal Swedish Air Force) 1960–1998 and Drakens have been exported to Denmark and Finland; Austria obtained

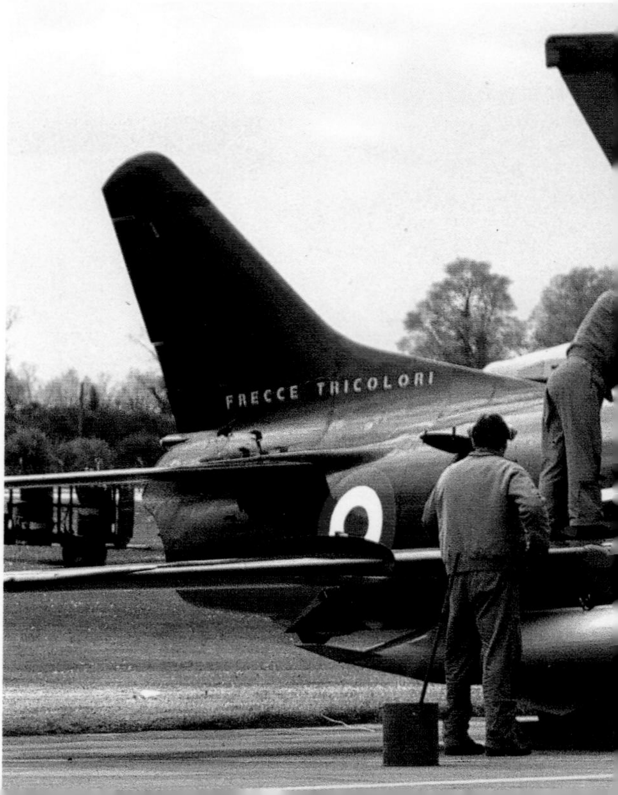

Left: Fiat G.91R of the Italian *Frecce Tricolori* aerobatic display team being refuelled prior to a display at RAF Mildenhall Air Fete in June 1979.

24 surplus Swedish J35Ds in 1985. Denmark's Drakens were extensively upgraded during the mid-1980s and the last was retired in December 1993. The Austrian Drakens will be progressively replaced by the Eurofighter from 2007.

Designed as a high-performance successor to the Draken with STOL capability from dispersed sites and able

Left: Eighteen C.8 and three CE.8 Starfighters (Canadair-built F-104Gs and Lockheed TF-104Gs respectively) served with the *Ejército del Aire* (Spanish Air Force), March 1955-May 1972. In May 1972 all 21 Spanish Starfighters were returned to the USAF for transfer to Greece (10) and Turkey (11). Spain joined NATO in 1982.

Below: Essentially a scaled-up version of the Dassault Mirage 2000, the 4000 prototype first flew on March 9, 1979, but its high cost associated with a twin-engined powerplant and advanced avionics led to the cancellation of the program in the 1980s. The prototype was used for a number of projects including the development of the M53-P2 engine required for the Rafale program.

Right: Dassault Mirage 2000s of the Armée de l'Air. The first of five 2000 prototypes flew on March 10, 1978 and the first production standard 2000C on November 20, 1982. Delivery of the Mirage 2000C single-seat interceptor began in April 1983 and eventually the type equipped three squadrons of the French air force. Production totalled 121 aircraft for France and Mirage 2000s were exported to Egypt, India, Peru, Abu Dhabi, and Greece.

Above: The Hawker Hunter was one of Britain's most successful post-war designs with production totalling 1,985 examples, including 445 built in Belgium and the Netherlands; 429 were exported as new aircraft, and in excess of 700 Hunters were refurbished or completely remanufactured for more than seventeen air forces. Among the users were Switzerland, India, and Chile. This Hunter, probably of the Omani air force, gives a new meaning to the concept of a "low" pass!

Above: An F-6 (Chinese Shenyang-built MiG-19SF) of the
Pakistan Air Force firing its nose mounted 30mm NR-30
cannons. F-6s were used by the PAF in the 1965 war with
India where their outstanding dogfight maneuverability
and tremendous hitting power (each 30mm projectile
having more than twice the kinetic energy of the Aden or
DEFA of similar caliber) proved highly valuable in combat
with IAF Hunters.

to fulfil a multitude of roles including attack, overland and overwater reconnaissance, and interceptor, the Saab 37 Viggen (Thunderbolt), can also operate from the close confines of small airfields and roads. The Draken's delta wing was retained but a canard foreplane with trailing

Left: F-104G-LO KF+134 of the Luftwaffe, which was issued to JaboG 31, crashed on July 30, 1969. The pilot, Hptm Achim Baumgardt, ejected safely. All told, the Luftwaffe lost 246 F-104s and 97 pilots and crew killed. The *Marineflieger* (West German Navy) lost 46 Starfighters and 23 pilots and crew killed.

Below: NF-5A K-3023, F-16A J-617, and F-104G Starfighter D-8282, one of 95 F/RF-104Gs built by Fokker, of the Royal Netherlands Air Force. Starfighters entered service with the Netherlands AF in December 1962 and the last were replaced by F-16A/Bs in November 1984.

Above left: Dassault Mirage IIIR2Z, a variant of the IIIR with a more powerful 15,873-lb thrust SNECMA Atar 9K-50 turbojet, of the South African Air Force. They were finally withdrawn from service in October 1990.

Below left: Dassault Mirage FICZs of No.3 Squadron, South African Air Force Strike Command, based at Waterkloof. The Mirage F.1CZ entered SAAF service in 1974 and was later supplemented by the Mirage F.1AZ for the air-ground role.

Below: Dassault Mirage F1JA (F.1E) of *Escuadrón de caza* 2112 of the Ecuador Air Force with a SEPECAT Jaguar International and IAI Kfir C2, one of 12 acquired in 1982. Altogether, Ecuador obtained 16 F1JA single-seaters and two F1JE two-seat trainers.

Previous page: The Belgian Air Force took delivery of Dassault Mirage 5BA ground attack aircraft (here with a Hawker Siddeley Buccaneer), Mirage 5BD two-seaters, and Mirage 5BR reconnaissance aircraft. Some were being upgraded with HUD, laser rangefinder and canards when all were retired in December 1993 for economic reasons.

Right: The MiG-25 (NATO name "Foxbat") was designed to counter the 1950s North American B-70 Valkyrie Mach 3 strategic cruise bomber design, which was eventually cancelled, The first of seven prototypes flew on September 9, 1964. This is an Indian AF example of the 1972 "Foxbat B" MiG-25RB. They were exported to Algeria, Bulgaria, India, Iraq, Libya, and Syria.

edge flaps were added, enabling take-off runs of only 1,600 feet on hard paved surfaces., In 1964 Saab was contracted to build 800 aircraft in four basic versions including the AJ.37 attack fighter, which was to equip six first-line squadrons. The Viggen prototype first flew on February 8, 1967 and the AJ.37 first flew in February 1971. By early

1980 it was obvious that Sweden needed a single-seat, single-engined all-weather fighter, attack and reconnaissance aircraft to succeed the Viggen. In 1982 Saab received contracts for five prototypes and 30 production aircraft, to be known as the JAS 39 Gripen (Griffin).

The Cold War Thaw
The quest for Air Dominance

Left: 2/Lt Robert S. Roth, pilot of an A-7 Corsair of the 112th Tactical Fighter Group, Pittsburgh ANG, prepares for take-off on a flight mission in July 1981 during Exercise "Sentry Castle 81." The A-7D is armed with a single M61A1 Vulcan 20-mm cannon, usually carries two AIM-7L Sidewinder missiles on forward fuselage hardpoints, and can carry up to 15,000 lb of air-to-surface missiles, bombs, cluster bombs, rockets, or gun pods on six underwing ordnance stations. The pilot sits far forward on the fuselage.

In February 1982 the U.S. presented the Soviet Union with a draft treaty based on President Ronald Reagan's "zero option" proposal to cancel Pershing II and ground-launched cruise missile deployments and for the Soviets to dismantle their SS-20, SS-4, and SS-5 missiles. The next day the Soviet Union counter-proposed a two-thirds cut in all U.S. and Soviet medium-range nuclear weapons in Europe by 1990. Elsewhere, diplomacy failed. From April 2 to June 14, 1982, the Falklands War between Britain and Argentina was fought in the South Atlantic. In the Persian Gulf, complete aerial superiority would be achieved in Operation *Desert Storm*; air dominance was next on the agenda.

The first Argentinian aircraft shot down in the Falklands conflict, a Mirage III, was destroyed on May 2 by an AIM-9L Sidewinder fired by an RAF pilot flying a Sea Harrier. (The prototype Mirage IIIE had first flown as early as December 17, 1956 and when production ceased in 1992 no less than 1,422 Mirage III, Mirage 5, and Mirage 50 aircraft had been built.) The first of 1 Squadron RAF's GR.3s flew a non-stop 9hr 15-min flight from St. Mawgan, England, to Wideawake airfield on Ascension Island on May 3. This record distance of 4,600 miles beat the previous record held by a single-engine V/STOL aircraft of 3,500 miles from London to New York, set during the May 1969 Daily Mail Transatlantic Air Race. (*Cont. page 277.*)

Above: A Libyan Su-22 "Fitter-J" armed with two AA-2 Atoll air-to-air missiles with a wing tank under each wing photographed by a U.S. Navy aircraft on an intercept mission over the southern Mediterranean near the coast of Libya on August 18, 1981 during a USN open ocean missile firing exercise.

Right: Three A-7D Corsairs of the 152nd Tactical Fighter Training Squadron, 162nd Tactical Fighter Training Wing of the Arizona ANG in September 1981. The Arizona ANG unit, which also operated F-100D/Fs until March 1978, began training A-7D pilots for the ANG in January 1977 and A-7Ds and A-7Ks were operated until March 1986 when conversion to F-16A/Bs began.

Right: Mirage 2000 armed with AM 39, the air-to-air version of the Exocet anti-ship, all weather, sea-skimming fire-and-forget missile. The frigate USS *Stark* was hit by two such missiles on May 17, 1987, while deployed to the Arabian Gulf. Only one of them exploded. The missiles were fired by an Iraqi aircraft, killing 37 sailors, wounding 21 others, and causing heavy damage. The Iraqis claimed that it was an accident.

Left: AV-8B Harriers of VMA-231 of the U.S. Marine Corps. The USMC first became interested in the aircraft in 1968 and advanced model of the Harrier was built as the McDonnell Douglas/BAe AV-8B with a new wing and uprated Pegasus 15 engine. The USMC took delivery of the first production aircraft in 1983. 280 single-seat and two-seat aircraft were built. Six additional attrition replacements were ordered following Operation *Desert Storm*, after seven were lost, mainly to SAMs, as the type was used in a low-level ground support role. The first Harrier GR.Mk.5, generally similar to the AV-8B, flew in April 1985 and 62 were ordered for the RAF. There were AV-8As for India and Spain, and AV-8B+ aircraft for Spain, Thailand, and the *Marina Militare Italiana* (MMI).

Some 28 Sea Harriers and RAF Harrier GR.Mk.3s operating from HMS *Hermes* and *Invincible* made 2,380 sorties and destroyed 27 Argentinian aircraft in air-to-air combat, without loss resulting from air-to-air combat.

By the mid-1980s the USN had in service twelve carrier air wings aboard the same number of carriers. Each air wing could muster eighty or more aircraft. One of the most important of these was the F-14 Tomcat, which had first gone to sea with the USN in October 1974. The Tomcat owed its origins to the F-111, originally the TFX (Tactical Fighter Experimental). The F-111 was originally planned to replace almost all fighter and attack aircraft in the USAF and US Navy. (*Cont. page 282*)

Left: During the Falklands War (Operation *Corporate*) in April–June 1982, Royal Navy Sea Harriers and RAF Harrier GR.3s armed with AIM-9L Sidewinders and operating from the two carriers won the crucial battle for air superiority against Argentine A-4 Skyhawks, Dagger fighter-bombers, and Mirage jets. Despite being outnumbered six to one, Sea Harriers flew 2,000 operational sorties and achieved 23 kills in air-to-air combat.

Right: These two USAF F-16As were among the first to be assigned to the 50th Tactical Fighter Wing at Hahn AB, West Germany, in July 1982, when transition as the first USAF F-16 wing was made. With the F-16 Hahn joined four European air forces and eight European air bases in operating Falcons for the defense of Europe.

Above: Royal Danish Air Force TF-104G at RAF Mildenhall in 1983. The TF-104G was the two-seat version of the F-104G. It lost the 20mm Vulcan cannon and center-line bomb rack of the single-seat fighter. All TF-104Gs were built by Lockheed, but some used components supplied by the European Starfighter consortium.

Right: F-15 Eagle 76119 firing an AIM-7 Sparrow missile in September 1982. The Eagle can now be armed with combinations of four different air-to-air weapons: the AIM-7 or AIM-120 medium range on the lower fuselage, AIM-9L/M Sidewinder or AIM-120 on two wing pylons, and internal Gatling 20mm in the right wing root.

In 1961 Secretary of Defense Robert McNamara recommended that the USAF and USN seriously consider combining their two missions—fleet air defense for the Navy and high Mach, low level interdiction for the air force—into one aircraft. Commonality was never reached. The 562 F-111s built were used as attack bombers in the USAF, while the overweight General Dynamics/Grumman developed F-111B, which at best would have given the USN a long-range interceptor, was cancelled in July 1968. In October 1967 Grumman had gone to the Navy with a proposal, recommending a way to wrap a new airframe around the existing F-111B weapons system and engines. The resulting decrease in weight fulfilled the fighter role of air superiority and in January 1969 the Defense Department awarded Grumman the contract for what had become known as the VFX. Thus the F-14 was born and the Tomcat flew for the first time on December 21, 1970. The rest, as they say, is history. Production of the Tomcat continued into the 1980s and a total of 26 front-line

Right: F-14A Tomcat of VF-211 "Fighting Checkmates" launching an AIM-54A Phoenix missile.

Left F-14A Tomcat of VF-51. Fighter Squadron 51 started changing to Tomcats from F-4s in 1978. The Screaming Eagles claim to be the first squadron to have landed the Tomcat automatically both by day and by night.

Above: F-14A Tomcat of the Imperial Iranian Air Force. Eighty F-14As were accepted by the U.S. Navy on behalf of the Imperial Iranian Air Force (IIAF) between December 1975 and July 1978. After the Shah was deposed in January 1979 the IIAF Tomcats were progressively cannibalized and others lost in the long war against Iraq.

Above: MiG-29 "Fulcrum" viewed from a RAF interceptor. The 1977 MiG-29 was designed as an agile counterair fighter with secondary attack capability, what the Soviets referred to as *Logkii frontovoi,* or "light frontline."

Right: F-14A Tomcats of VF-84 from the USS *Nimitz*. Like VF-51, the bearers of the "skull and crossbones" transitioned from the F-4.

and four second-line squadrons were eventually equipped with the F-14A. The Sixth Fleet, in the Mediterranean, proved an efficient avenger, and then deterrent, in the fight against international terrorism with raids against Libyan and Lebanese targets. In February 1986 *Operation Prairie Fire* was launched to provoke Libya into a direct military confrontation.

On April 14–15, 1986 Operation *El Dorado Canyon*, the bombing of terrorist-related targets at Tripoli and Benghazi, went ahead. USAFE F-111F/EF-111A Ravens

Right: Phantom of No.74 "Tiger" Squadron in superb color scheme. On October 19, 1984 No.74 "Tiger" Squadron reformed at Wattisham to fly 15 refurbished ex-U.S. F-4J (UK) Phantoms to fill a gap caused by the need to deploy UK-based FGR.2s to the Falklands. Early in January 1991 the F-4Js of No.74 Squadron were withdrawn and replaced by the FGR.2s released by RAF Leuchars.

Right: Ex-DDR Sukhoi Su-20 "Fitter."

based in Britain, and USN carrier-borne A-7E Corsairs, F/A-18A Hornets and A-6Es in the eastern Mediterranean struck at terrorist-related targets in Libya in Tripoli and in and around Benghazi. Operation *Praying Mantis* against Iranian naval vessels in the Arabian Gulf went ahead on April 18–19, 1988.

In 1988, existence of the F-117A Stealth, the first production combat type designed to exploit low-observable (LO) technology was officially revealed. "Not since the Manhattan Project," said Defense Secretary Frank

Left: MiG-29 "Fulcrum" of the former DDR, the type retained by Germany after reunification in 1990 and used to equip 731 *Staffel* of JG 73 Steinhoff at Laage. This unit will eventually convert to the Eurofighter Typhoon and all MiG-29s will be retired or transferred to the Polish air force.

Below: MiG-23 of former DDR. Development of the MiG-23 "Flogger" single-seat multi-role tactical fighter began during the early 1960s. The Model 23-11 had a variable-geometry wing planform and a single engine.

Carlucci, "have we seen a program cloaked in such secrecy." The same year the Intermediate-Range Nuclear Forces Treaty was mandated by the first elimination of an entire weapons class from U.S. and Soviet inventories.

January 1989 saw political upheaval in Eastern Europe that ended 45 years of Soviet domination. On November 9, 1989 the German Democratic Republic opened the Berlin Wall, and on October 3, 1990 Germany was reunified after 45 years of partition.

Meanwhile, during December 20, 1989 to January 1, 1990, Panama was invaded by U.S. forces in Operation *Just Cause*. Four F-16s and 16 F-15s patrolled the waters between Panama and Cuba throughout the operation. At the beginning of the invasion, two F-117As—in a small-scale "shock and awe" version of the threatened but undelivered tactic of the later war in Iraq—dropped two 2,000-lb bombs close to the barracks of the 6th and 7th Rifle Companies of the Panama Defense Force at Rio Hato

in an attempt to stun and confuse. Soon afterward, Rangers, and Paratroopers of the 82nd Airborne parachuted in.

Conflict in the Persian Gulf began on August 1, 1990, when Iraq's president Saddam Hussein's armies invaded

Right: MiG-23 "Flogger" of the Polish Air Force. The MiG-23-11 flew for the first time on April 10, 1967 and fifty were built between mid-1969 and the end of 1970, before production switched to the MiG-23M series.

Kuwait. On August 7 President Bush ordered Operation *Desert Shield* to liberate Kuwait. USAF Lt. Gen. Charles A. Homer, the allied coalition's supreme air commander, began coordinating all air actions related to the buildup and within days established HQ Central Command Air

Forces (Forward) in Saudi Arabia. Five USAF fighter squadrons, a contingent of AWACs and part of the 82nd Airborne Division moved into the theater within five days. In total, 25 fighter squadrons flew non-stop to the theater. Within 35 days the USAF deployed a fighter force that equaled Iraq's fighter capability in numbers. The Coalition built an air force of 2,350 aircraft, over half of which were combat aircraft.

On January 16–17 Operation *Desert Storm* began with more than 40 F-117A Nighthawk Stealth Fighters attacking top-priority targets in Iraq. They were the only aircraft to bomb strategic

Left: The first four production models of the F-16 (F-16A, F-16B, F-16C, and F-16D) displayed by the 58th Tactical Fighter Wing (58th Fighter Wing from October 1991) on the flight line at Luke AFB, Arizona. The Wing began receiving the F-16A in 1983 and the F-16C in 1984.

Above: English Electric (BAC) Lightning T5 XS417, which first flew on July 17, 1964 and last flew on May 18, 1987. It was the only all-British supersonic fighter/interceptor (1,011 mph, Mach 1.5 at 36,000ft).

Left: Pre-flighting an A-7E Corsair on the flight deck of the USS *Saratoga* (CV-60) prior to flight operations in February 1986. Powerplant is Allison TF412-A-2.

targets such as aircraft shelters and bunkers in Baghdad and did so using 2,000-lb GBU-27 laser-guided bombs. Without Stealth, a typical strike mission would require 32 aircraft with bombs, 16 fighter escorts, eight "Wild Weasel" aircraft to suppress enemy radar, four aircraft to electronically jam enemy radar, and 15 tankers to refuel them. With Stealth technology, the same mission needed no more than eight F-117As and two tankers to refuel them. *(Cont. page 307)*

Left: McDonnell (now Boeing) F-18 Hornets of the USN *Blue Angels*. The display team unveiled their new jets for the first time on November 8, 1986, the 40th anniversary of the team. Since 1946, it is estimated that some 380 million people have watched the displays.

Left: McDonnell Douglas CE.15 (EF-18 Hornet) of the *Ejército del Aire* (Spanish Air Force), which achieved initial operational capability with the C-15 single-seat and CE-15 two-seat Hornet in 1987.

Above: F.6 Lightning AM and Tornado F.3 ZE292/CA of No.5 Squadron RAF, in December 1987.

Previous page: McDonnell Douglas F/A-18 Hornet in June 1988. Hornets have been bought by Canada, Australia, Finland, Kuwait, Malaysia, and Switzerland.

Right: An F-14A Tomcat of VF-143 clears the leading edge of the angled flight deck of the nuclear-powered aircraft carrier USS *Dwight D. Eisenhower* (CVN-69) in the Mediterranean after being launched from the No. 4 waist catapult in early 1988.

F-117s flew more than 1,250 sorties and dropped more than 2,000 tons of bombs during *Desert Storm*. F-4Gs were deployed to Saudi Arabia in support of the operation and on that first mission, shortly after midnight, F-4Gs of the 52nd TFS carrying HARM anti-radiation missiles flew as part of the package.

The coalition air forces faced 750 Iraqi combat aircraft, 200 support aircraft, Scud surface-to-surface missiles, chemical and biological weapon capability, "state-of-the-art" air defenses, 10 types of surface-to-air missiles, around 9,000 anti-aircraft artillery pieces and thousands of small arms. The Iraqi Air Force had 24 main operating bases and 30 dispersal fields; many equipped with the latest in hardened aircraft shelters. Iraq had more tanks than Great Britain and Germany combined.

Coalition aircraft "surgically" bombed key Iraqi military targets such as heavily

Right: USAFE General Dynamics F-16 Fighting Falcon from Spangdahlem passing a German *schloss*. Spangdahelm AB is one of four airbases around the world that have the F-16 Mini D Wild Weasel. The others are Misawa AB Japan, Shaw AFB South Carolina, and Mountain Home AFB Idaho. All of these aircraft have HTS pods (Harm Targeting System) mounted on the starboard chin station.

fortified command and communications centers, missile launch sites, radar facilities and airports and runways. Iraqi ground forces were under heavy day-and-night air attack from that day on. Within 10 days of offensive operations, air sorties reached the 10,000 mark. The coalition's intensive airpower had crippled or destroyed Iraq's nuclear, biological, and chemical weapons development programs,

its air defenses, its offensive air and ballistic missile capability, and its internal state control mechanisms.

U.S. forces had Global Positioning System navigation available in three dimensions for 20 hours each day and in two dimensions 24 hours a day in *Desert Shield/Storm*. Despite featureless terrain, GPS allowed accurate navigation to targets. From January 16 until February 27,

Left:. U.S. Navy A-7E Corsairs of VA-46 attached to CVW-7 (Carrier Air Wing Seven) in formation over the carrier USS *Dwight D. Eisenhower* in the Mediterranean in July 1988. The IKE/CVW-7 Battle Group was the first in theater to deter Iraqi aggression in Operation *Desert Shield*.

four USAF AWACs aircraft were continuously airborne,
controlling more than 3,000 coalition sorties each day.
Two JointSTARS (USAF-Grumman Joint Surveillance
Target Attack Radar System) test aircraft flew 54 combat
sorties supporting all mission tasking. One of the two was
in the air every day, tracking every vehicle that moved on
the ground. JointSTARS identified and targeted Scud
missiles and launchers, convoys, trucks, tanks, surface-to-
air missile sites, and artillery pieces for coalition aircraft.

Some 120 F-15C/D Eagles deployed to the Gulf and
flew more than 5,900 sorties. Every Iraqi fixed-wing
aircraft destroyed in air-to-air combat, including five
Soviet-made MiG-29 Fulcrums, was downed by F-15Cs.

Right: Mirage IIIO of the
Royal Australian Air Force
in national colors. Australia
acquired 100 Mirage IIIOs.

No coalition aircraft were lost to Iraqi fighters. Forty-eight F-15Es deployed flew more than 2,200 sorties for the loss of only two in combat. F-15Es used the LANTIRN navigation and targeting pods with spectacular results. The USAF's 249 F-16 Fighting Falcons flew more than 13,450 sorties—more than any other aircraft in the Gulf War by day and night and in all weathers. They attacked Iraqi equipment in Kuwait and southern Iraq, flew missions against Scud missiles and launchers, and destroyed interdiction targets such as military production and support, chemical production facilities, and airfields. In all the USAF flew 59 percent of all sorties with 50 percent of the aircraft and had 37 percent of the losses. Pilots used

precision-guided munitions such as GBU-27, GBU-12 and GBU-24 laser-guided bombs, and GBU-15 electro-optical glide bombs, with deadly effectiveness, dropping 7,400 tons. They were responsible for approximately 90 percent of the total PGMs dropped. USAF fighters destroyed 36 of the 39 Iraqi fixed-wing aircraft and helicopters shot down during *Desert Storm*. AGM-65 Maverick missiles were employed by F-16s (and A-l0s) to attack armored targets. The radar-guided AIM-7 Sparrow proved to be the most potent air-to-air weapon. USAF-launched Sparrows downed 22 Iraqi fixed-wing aircraft and three helicopters. Although the

Left: Mirage IIIO of the Royal Australian Air Force taxi-ing out at RAAF Richmond near Sydney during the Bicentennial Air Show in 1988. In 1990 Pakistan purchased 50 of the Australian Mirages after the RAAF retired the survivors of its fleet.

Above: F-16 of the USAF *Thunderbirds* at the Abbotsford International Air Show, Canada, in August 1989.

Right: An F-14A Tomcat prepares to touch down on the flight deck of the nuclear-powered aircraft carrier USS *Carl Vinson* at dusk in October 1988.

Previous page: Mirage IIIS of the Swiss Air Force at Dubendorf, Switzerland, in 1990. In all, Switzerland received 36 Mirage IIIS and 18 Mirage IIIRS aircraft, which were later fitted with new avionics and canards. On October 22, 1999, Switzerland retired its Mirage IIIS fighters while its Mirage IIIRS reconnaissance and Mirage IIIBS/BD trainers remained in service until at least 2003.

Right: CAF CF-5A 116703 at Abbottsford International Air Show in 1989. Canadair built CF-5A/D single-seat and two-seat Freedom fighters and NF-5A/B aircraft for the Canadian and Netherlands air forces respectively.

F-14D (A+) Tomcat with advanced avionics and weapons systems and more powerful engines arrived too late to see action, eight F-14A and two F-14B squadrons were deployed aboard five carriers. On January 21, 1991 an F-14B and an F/A-18C were lost to SAMs. USN aviation claimed three victories in the Gulf War. Iraq lost 90 aircraft to coalition air forces, 39 of them in air-to-air combat; six

were lost in accidents; 16 aircraft were captured or destroyed by coalition ground forces; and 122 were flown to Iran, a confirmed total loss of 234 aircraft. Of Iraq's 594 hardened aircraft shelters, 375 were damaged or destroyed by coalition bombing. It is estimated that 141 aircraft were destroyed in these shelters. By February 25, 1991, airpower had forced thousands of Iraqi soldiers to

abandon their stockpiles of equipment, weapons, and ammunition, and surrender. On February 7 Kuwait was liberated, although it was not until April 11 that the conflict was declared officially over.

Aerial superiority once again had been instrumental in an early victory, but by 1991 even air superiority was out-dated. In 1996 William J. Perry, U.S. Secretary of Defense, declared that: "For decades we've described our objective as air superiority. In *Desert Storm* what we had was not air superiority but air dominance." *(Cont. page 332)*

Left: Northrop F-5E/F Tiger IIs of the Swiss Air Force at Dubendorf, Switzerland in 1990. Tiger IIs, like the F-5 Freedom Fighter before it, served many overseas air forces and were license-built by Canadair, South Korea, and Taiwan. In Switzerland the Tiger II was built by the Federal Aircraft Factory under license for the Swiss Air Force.

Right: Warsaw Pact was never like this! Aircraft like this Ex-DDR (German People's Republic) Sukhoi Su-20 "Fitter," which were formerly operated by the air force, the LSK (*Luftstreitkräfte*) and the LV (*Luftverteidigung*, air defense) were absorbed into the German air force after the Berlin Wall came down in November 1989, tested, and later scrapped. Only the MiG-29s were incorporated into the German Air Force in 1990–91 after reunification.

Below: F-16 Fighting Falcon of 8th TFW at Kunsan AB, Korea, in 1990.

Previous page: Ex-East German air force MiG-21 in German Air Force markings. Large numbers of MiG-21R, MiG-21M and MiG-21MF warplanes remain in service, including many with the non-Soviet air forces of the former Warsaw Pact.

Above: MiG-21 in North Vietnamese Air Force colors taxi-ing in at Oshkosh, Wisconsin, in 1990.

Right: MiG-21 of JG.1. The Soviets had planned to replace the ageing MiG-21s at Holzdorf AB with MiG-29s. As German reunification approached, the Soviets stopped further sales, but it did not matter. What had been a state-of-the-art piece of secret Soviet technology simply becme part of the NATO inventory.

"We liked it and we want to continue to have it…Do not take people seriously when they tell you 'We do not need advanced fighters like the F-22 and the F/A-18 because we will not face advanced fighters.'" He was not looking for an equal fight. "We want to be unfair," he said. "We want the advantage to be wholly and completely on our side."

Right: Shark-mouthed MiG-21 22+02 of the German Air Force. The MiG-21M, built in Moscow for export during 1968–71, was also built under license by HAL (Hindustan Aeronautics Ltd) in India,

The high-technology Lockheed Martin YF-22 Raptor, which in April 1991 won the competitive evaluation with the Northrop/McDonnell Douglas YF-23 prototype, is the first of the so-called "air dominance" fighters. Raptor will counter multiple defense threats such as the advanced integrated air defence system (IADS), fighters, cruise

Previous page: F/A-18 Hornets formate on the camera ship and the back-seater cameraman. The larger McDonnell-Douglas (Boeing from 1997) F/A-18E Super Hornet development of the F/A-18C was produced to fill the gap left by the cancellation in 1991 of the General Dynamics/McDonnell Douglas A-12 Avenger II carrier-borne attack warplane.

Above: The existence of the F-117A was not revealed officially until November 1988 and its first operational deployment was to Panama just after midnight on December 20, 1989 when six F-117As supported Operation *Just Cause*. The F-117 is expected to remain in USAF service until the 2020s

Left: F-117A Stealth Fighter in May 1991. Development and manufacture (starting with five full-scale development F-117As) began simultaneously in November 1978 within a highly classified environment.

Left: McDonnell F-15C Eagles of the 33rd TFW. The nearest aircraft, 85-0099, was flown by Capt Lawrence E. "Cherry" Pitts of the 58th TFS "Gorillas" on January 19, 1991 when he destroyed a MiG-25 with an AIM-7 missile.

missiles, theater ballistic missile (TBM) sites and weapons of mass destruction. The Raptor's unique combination of stealth technology, supercruise (ability to cruise at supersonic speed without using its afterburners), maneuverability and integrated avionics enables 24-hour stealth operations across the spectrum of missions. It has a maximum level speed of 900 mph-plus at sea level and a range of more than 2,000 miles and is armed with an internal M61A2 20mm gun, two AIM-9 Sidewinders stored internally in the side weapons bays, six AIM-120 AMRAMs in the main weapons bay, and approximately eight SBDs internally. For ground attack two 1,000 lb JDAMs replace the four AMRAAMs internally. The USAF has plans for a fleet of 339 Raptors (now designated the F/A-22) with a requirement for at least 381, to operate with ACC, AETC and AFMC.

Far left: Phantoms of No.74 "Tiger" Squadron at RAF Mildenhall Air Show in 1992. On January 1, 1993 No.74 Squadron disbanded.

Below: The Lockheed Martin F-22 Raptor single-seat fighter first flew on September 29, 1990 (YF-22A prototype) and in April 1991 won the competitive evaluation with the Northrop/ McDonnell Douglas YF-23 prototype.

21st Century Fighters

Typhoon, JSF, and Electronic Warfare

Left: Close up of the intake area of the Harrier VTOL jump jet. VTOL and STOVL were still important considerations for the latest fighter configurations.

In 1996 U.S. Air Force Secretary Sheila E. Widnall warned that "Nations around the world have caught up with us in technology and the Air Force has to expect to face advanced weapons in the future." Beginning in the Fifties the U.S. initiated some very successful and lucrative co-assembly and license manufacture programs in Canada and Europe, and thousands of F-86, F-104, and F-16 aircraft equipped NATO air arms. Early in 1988 however, it was revealed that the next fighter to equip four, and possibly more NATO nations, would be Eurofighter, an aircraft built wholly in Europe.

An overall production contract for the initial purchase of 620 Eurofighter single seat air combat fighter aircraft (now Eurofighter Typhoon), with a further option for 90 aircraft, was signed by the NATO Eurofighter and Tornado Management Agency (NETMA). Production called for 232 aircraft for the RAF, 180 for the Luftwaffe in Germany, 121 for the *Aeronautica Militate Italiana* (AMI) or Italian Air Force and 87 for the *Ejército del Aire* (Spanish Air Force) with manufacture being completed at four assembly lines in the partner nations. Power is provided by two EJ200 turbofan engines manufactured by Eurojet (Rolls-Royce in the UK, MTU in Germany, Fiat Avio in Italy and SENER (now ITP) in Spain).

From the outset the entire aircraft was designed around one of the most advanced cockpit environments ever

Above: *Sevasti Tovarich!* Sukhoi Su 27 "Flanker" on finals at Farnborough.

Left: MiG-29 "Fulcrum" of the Czech Air Force in 1992.

developed, which enables a single pilot to position the aircraft, manipulate the sensors, and deploy the weapons. Other notable features include a combination of automated defensive systems, advanced sensors, datalink technology and data fusion, and a complex fly-by-wire system, which is essential to give the aircraft outstanding maneuverability.

The DA.1, the first Eurofighter 2000 prototype completed in Germany flew on March 27, 1994, and was followed on April 6, 1994 by DA.2, the Eurofighter 2000 prototype completed in the UK. However, financial and technical problems and political and strategic reviews dogged development of Eurofighter Typhoon, which is of vital importance to the future of British, German, Italian and Spanish air defense, and deliveries lagged behind schedule. The first two Eurofighter 2000 prototypes, completed in Germany and the UK as DA.1 and DA.2 respectively, first flew on March 27 and April 6, 1994; and the Italian, German, and British-built IPA production

aircraft all flew for the first time in April 2002. In the RAF the Typhoon will first replace the Tornado F.Mk.3 and then the Jaguar. In Germany Eurofighter will replace the Luftwaffe's MiG-29, F-4F Phantom and Tornado aircraft. (Germany plans to reduce its fighter force from 426

Left: Raw power! Single seat Dassault Rafale taking off on re-heat. The Rafale is a two-seat *Avion de Combat Tactique* (French Air Force) or single-seat *Avion de Combat Marine* (French Navy) interceptor, multirole fighter and reconnaissance aircraft. It was first ordered at the beginning of the 1990s to replace French Air Force Jaguars, and Navy Crusaders and Super Etendards.

Above: MiG-29K multi-role naval fighter with folding outer portions of the wing pictured at Moscow Airshow in 1992. The aircraft was rejected by the Russian authorities in favor of the Su-27K, but India has purchased the MiG-29K.

aircraft to 265 by 2015). Italy plans to convert five *gruppi* (squadrons) to the Eurofighter.

Meanwhile, on October 24, 2000, the Lockheed Martin XF35A (Joint Strike Fighter (JSF) demonstrator flew for the first time. it has been designed and built to give the USAF an affordable conventional attack aircraft with stealth, advanced avionics, and low life-cycle and operational costs, together with high reliability and good range, speed, and warload. A U.S. Navy requirement for CV (carrier) operation is similar, but has bigger wings for low-speed carrier approaches, as well as heavier landing

Above: F-15E Strike Eagles of the 492nd TFS, 78th TFW on a sortie from RAF Lakenheath, England, to Germany in June 1995. The first F-15E Strike Eagle flew on December 11, 1986. F-15Es had additional avionics and increased air-to-ground weapon load.

gear and an arresting hook for carrier landings. JSF will also give the USMC and the Royal Navy an advanced attack aircraft with excellent STOVL (Short takeoff, vertical landing) characteristics for operation from forward battlefield areas, or the smaller Marine helicopter carriers and British "jump jet" carriers. The JAST also has to perform a secondary air-defense mission, using air-to-air missiles (AAMs) to defend itself, or to protect fleet assets from airborne intruders.

High performance was not a requirement for the JSF, though of course it was desirable. (*Cont page 354.*)

Right: *Thunderbirds* are go! F-16s of the famous USAF display team at RAF Mildenhall, England in 1997. The list of aircraft flown by the Air Demonstration Squadron since its activation in 1953 is a mini fighter history in itself: F-84 Thunderjet, F-84F Thunderstreak, F-100 Super Sabre, F-105 Thunderchief, back to the F-100, F-4E Phantom, T-38 Talon, (a step down prompted by the oil crisis), then in 1983 the F-16 Fighting Falcon, and in 1992 the F-16C.

An F/A-18C Hornet of VFA-81 from the USS *Enterprise* conducting training with a Russian built MiG-29 "Fulcrum" of the German Air Force during joint operations conducted from July 31 to August 13, 1996.

Performance was specified to be comparable to existing F-16s and F/A-18s operating in the strike role, though any incidental improvements in performance were welcome. This multi-role fighter, which resembles a single-engined version of the F-22 Raptor, though it also has a high degree of stealthy contouring, will be able to operate in both the

Above: MiG-23ML of the
Czechoslovak Air Force.
The MiG-23ML was also
exported to East
Germany, Syria, and North
Korea.

Left: F-4F Phantom 31+61
of JG 74 of the Luftwaffe
celebrating 35 years
continuous service in
1996.

STOVL and CTOL (Conventional take-off and landing)
roles. The STOVL version features a vertically mounted
"lift fan" behind the cockpit, driven by a shaft off the
P&W F119 engine, plus a vectored exhaust and two
exhaust ducts, extending from each side of the engine to
exit in the bottom of the wings. For the CTOL
(Conventional take-off and landing) and CV (carrier)
variants, the lift fan is deleted and replaced with additional
fuel tanks. The wings and tail are smaller for the CTOL
version. The lift fan approach has the advantage that it
minimizes hot exhaust ingestion back into the engine, a
common problem with STOVL designs that robs them of
vertical thrust. The arrangement is similar to that
pioneered by the Yakovlev Yak-141 Freestyle STOVL
fighter, which did not enter production. In addition to its
advanced stealth design, JSF incorporates maneuverability,

Left: *Turk Hava Kuvvetleri* (*THK*, Turkish Air Force) Northrop F-5 of the Turkish Stars aerobatic display team taxies past at RAF Mildenhall, England, in May 1998. Turkey occupies a strategic position on Europe's southern flank and was an early member of NATO. From 1965, the Turkish Air Force received 75 F-5As, 20 RF-5As, and 13 F-5Bs through MAP. Following the Turkish invasion of Cyprus in 1974, U.S. aid was temporarily suspended. With NATO assistance restored, large numbers of surplus F-5s were transferred. The *THK* is now looking to replace the aging Freedom Fighters with F-16A/Bs over time.

long range, and highly advanced avionics and weapons systems that will permit simultaneous engagement of multiple targets in enemy airspace.

The X-35A demonstrator first flew on October 24, 2000, and in late 2001 was declared winner of the concept demonstration phase (CDP) in competition with the Boeing X-32A. Lockheed Martin expects to build 3,000 JSFs, including 1,763 F-35A CTOL variants for the USAF, 609 F-35B STOVL variants for the USMC, 480 F-35C CV

Left: An F/A-18 Hornet of VFA-87 soars over the fields of Sardinia, Italy, in May 1997. VFA-87 was deployed to the Mediterranean aboard the aircraft carrier USS *John F. Kennedy.*

Below: A yellow jacketed flight-director motions away Modex 202, a "Tophatter" F-14A immediately after landing aboard the USS *John F. Kennedy* in the Mediterranean in October 1997.

variants for the USN, and 150 for the Royal Navy. The remainder are likely to be the F-35C CV variant. A final decision on British JCA production will not be made until a firm decision whether to build two new carriers to go into RN service in the next decade is made. They would

Right: A red-coated ordnancemen attends to the port AIM-9L Sidewinder IR-homing missile, as other ordnancemen and a green-jacketed maintainer (aircraft and catapult) of VF-14 direct a "Tophatter" Tomcat along the deck of the USS *John F. Kennedy* after landing.

have to be built to handle STOVL aircraft, but would be designed to accommodate catapult and arresting gear in case a decision is taken to operate fixed-wing aircraft as well. USAF is developing the JSF to replace its current force of F-16s and A-10s that will comprise the bulk of the

Above: "Black Aces" F-14A Tomcat and a F/A-18C Hornet of VFA-15 "Valions" on the waist cats aboard the *Kennedy*.

USAF's fighter fleet for up to 50 years. The U.S. Marine Corps will use the JSF to replace its AV-8B Harrier II aircraft in the STOVL attack role and its F/A-18C/D Hornet fighters and the USN wants JSF to replace its F/A-18C/D Hornets. The NATO air campaign against

Yugoslavia over Kosovo in the spring of 1999 revealed a shortfall in electronic warfare (EW) capabilities. EW missions during the Kosovo campaign relied heavily on the venerable EA-6B Prowler, and Prowler crews were stretched to the limit. (*Cont. page 369.*)

Previous page: Sukhoi SU-22 M4 "Fitter-K" of the 8th Tactical Fighter Squadron, Polish Air Force from Miroslawiec. This heavy and not very maneuverable aircraft evolved from the Sukhoi SU-7, a short-range interceptor that gradually transferred to a ground-attack role in the 1970s.

Right: Saab 37 Viggen (Thunderbolt) of the Swedish air force Designed as a high-performance successor to the Draken, with STOL capability from dispersed sites. The Viggen is able to fulfil a multitude of roles, including attack, overland and overwater reconnaissance, and interceptor. Pictured is a SK 37 tandem two-seat operational conversion trainer variant of the AJ 37. The periscope device is for the occupant of the rear cockpit.

Right: SAAB Viggen, easily identifiable by its large double-delta wing and canard foreplanes. In 1964 Saab was contracted to build 800 aircraft in four basic versions including the AJ.37 attack fighter, which was to equip six first line squadrons. The first Viggen prototype flew on February 8, 1967 and the AJ.37 in February 1971. The first of 149 JA 37 dedicated interceptor versions, which was designed as the successor to the AJ.37, entered service in 1979. In 1991 Saab began conversion of 115 existing Viggens to AJS 37 standard to create an interchangeable air defense attack and reconnaissance fighter. The the first of these began service entry in 1993.

The F-35 is now being seriously considered as an EW aircraft to supplement and eventually replace the Prowler. In Britain the JSF or the "Joint Combat Aircraft (JCA)", as it is known, will form an element of the "Future Offensive Aircraft System (FOAS)." The Royal Navy wants a next-generation STOVL fighter to replace its Sea Harriers and the RAF will need to replace its Harrier GR.7/9s. While Britain has committed to the STOVL F-35B as a Harrier replacement, the requirement is for 60–90 aircraft.

The continuing need for stealth technology was evidenced again when in March 2003 Operation *Iraqi Freedom*, the Second Gulf War, began with Coalition aircraft conducting strikes to prepare the battlefield. On March 20, six U.S. warships in the Persian Gulf and Red Sea, and two F-117 Stealth Fighters with no jamming or fighter support attacked leadership targets of opportunity in Baghdad.

The F-117s dropped four EGBU-27 LGBs and the warships fired more than 40 Tomahawk Land Attack (Cruise) Missiles. Next day coalition air forces commenced nearly 1,000 strike sorties marking the beginning of A-Day, the air campaign. Coalition forces seized an airfield in western Iraq and advanced 100 miles into Iraq. Over the

first three weeks of the war USAF crews flew nearly 40 percent of the combat sorties and delivered two-thirds of the munitions tonnage. The rest was divided between the USN, USMC, RAF, and RAAF. In all, 15,000 precision guided munitions were dropped and 750 cruise missiles were launched. In contrast to the 1991 war, when nine out

Left: By the early 1980s it was obvious that Sweden needed a single-seat, single-engined all-weather fighter to succeed the Viggen. In 1982 Saab received contracts for five prototypes and 30 production aircraft to be known as the JAS 39 *Gripen* (Griffin). By 1984 orders had risen to 350 to be delivered to the Swedish Air Force by 2001. Currently the requirement is for 218 Gripens, of which 190 are JAS 39A single-seaters and 28 JAS 39B two-seaters. On February 4, 2003 Hungary ordered JAS 39C/Ds, and on December 12, 2003 the Czech Air Force leased 14 new JAS 39s.

of ten expended weapons were unguided "dumb" bombs, about 75 percent of the weapons were precision-guided. From the outset combat aircraft patrolled "kill boxes" in southern and western Iraq searching for theater ballistic missiles. Aircraft like F-15Es, F-16s and other Coalition fighters soon destroyed Iraqi armor tracked by JointSTARS radar aircraft. During the war seven coalition fixed-wing aircraft were lost. In the months leading up to the war aircraft patrolling Iraqi "no-fly" zones bombed 80 air defense sites and by March 25, U.S. Defense Chief Donald H. Rumsfeld could claim "total dominance of the air." On April 9 Baghdad fell and on

Right: In 1988 the contract for the purchase of 620 Eurofighter Typhoons, and a further option for 90 aircraft, was signed by the NATO Eurofighter and Tornado Management Agency (NETMA).

Above: Tornado F.3s of 56 (Reserve) Squadron at RAF Coningsby, England, in May 2000. The Eurofighter Typhoon will first replace the Tornado F.Mk 3 and then the Jaguar.

Left: The Lockheed Martin F35 Joint Strike Fighter (JSF) is in effect three different aircraft based on common technology and is therefore one of the most ambitious aircraft programs in the history of aviation.

April 16 CENTCOM officials declared the end of major combat action in Iraq.

Air superiority has been the aim of commanders of warring nations since the Battle of Britain in 1940, during the Pacific battles of 1942-1945, again in Korea 1950-53, and in the Gulf Wars. Even at the beginning of the 21st Century, air power alone still cannot achieve total victory, though one day Air Dominance fighters just might.

Fighters Timeline

Early 1935 first flight of the Messerschmitt Bf 109 prototype

May 1935 first flight of the Curtiss Hawk 75 prototype. Deliveries of P-40 versions reach 13,738

November 6, 1935 prototype Hawker Hurricane flies for first time

March 5, 1936 first flight of the Supermarine Spitfire prototype

May 12, 1936 first flight of the Messerschmitt Bf 110 prototype day/night fighter

1936-38 Spanish Civil War

April 25, 1937 Guernica in northern Spain destroyed by German aircraft

1937 Sino (Chinese)-Japanese War begins

August 11, 1937 First flight of the Boulton Paul Defiant gun turreted fighter prototype

October 12, 1937 first flight of the Hawker Hurricane I production model

July 1938 first flight of the Spitfire Mk.1 production fighter. Total Spitfire production reaches 20,334 aircraft and 2,556 Seafires are also built

January 25, 1939 first flight of the XP-38 Lightning

March 30, 1939 *Flugkapitan* Hans Dieterle in a Heinkel He 100V-8 sets a new world air speed record of 463.92 mph at Oranienburg, Germany to beat the previous fastest speed of 440.69 mph set by Lt Francesco Agello in a Macchi MC 72 on October 23, 1934

March 1939 first flight of the Yakovlev Yak-1. Some 37,000 Yak 1-9 fighters were delivered to the Soviet air force by 1945

April 1, 1939 first flight of the Mitsubishi A6M Zero-Sen (Type 00 fighter). Total production reached 10,937 aircraft

April 26, 1939 *Flugkapitan* Fritz Wendel sets a new world air speed record of 469.22 mph in a Messerschmitt Bf 209V at Augsburg, Germany

June 1, 1939 First flight of the Focke Wulf Fw 190 prototype. Altogether, 20,051 Fw 190s were delivered

July 17, 1939 first flight of the Bristol Beaufighter prototype

August 27, 1939 Heinkel He 178 propelled by a gas turbine engine, first jet-powered aircraft to fly

September 1, 1939 Germany invades Poland

November 25, 1939 XP-39B Airacobra prototype with engine mounted in rear fuselage flies

December 1, 1939 a Fokker D XXI fighter of the Finnish Air Force destroyed by his own AA guns is the first loss suffered by the Finns in the "Winter War" with the Soviet Union. Another Fokker D XXI claims the first aerial victory (a SB-2 bomber)

February 1940 Blackburn Roc enters service with the FAA

May 15, 1941 first flight of the Gloster E.28/39 powered by a single 860 lb thrust Whittle W.1 turbojet

May 29, 1940 F4U Corsair, at the time the most powerful navy fighter in the world, first flies

June 11, 1940 first flight of the Hawker Hurricane II

June 1940 Fairey Fulmar becomes the first 8-gun fighter to enter service with the Fleet Air Arm

July 10–October 31 1940 Battle of Britain

October 26, 1940 North American P-51 Mustang flies

April 2, 1941 German He 280V-1, the first aircraft designed as a jet fighter, flies

April 18, 1941 first flight of the Me 262

May 6, 1941 XP-47B, precursor of the P-47 Thunderbolt, flies

June 22, 1941 Operation *Barbarossa*, German invasion of Russia, begins

September 1941 Hawker Typhoon enters service

October 2, 1941 H. Dittmar in a Bf 163 Komet sets new progressive air-launched record of 623.00 mph

December 7, 1941 Japanese attack on Pearl Harbor in the Hawaiian Islands brings the U.S. into the war with Japan. Germany declares war on the U.S.

1941 American Volunteer Group (AVG) "Flying Tigers" formed, inflicting heavy losses on Japanese bombers in September flying obsolete P-40Bs (**picture, opposite right**)

March 1942 Spitfire Mk V (**picture, opposite left**) is first Spitfire to serve overseas, flying out of Malta

May 7–9, 1942 Battle of the Coral Sea

May 29, 1942 Commonwealth CA-12 Boomerang flies.

May 31, 1942 de Havilland Mosquitoes fly their first sortie of the war

June 4–7, 1942 Battle of Midway

June 26, 1942 Grumman Hellcat flies

July 18, 1942 first flight of the Me 262 with turbojet engines

October 1, 1942 first flight of the Bell XP-59A Airacomet

November 15, 1942 He 219 Uhu (Owl) night-fighter flies in prototype form

January 8, 1944 Lockheed P-80 (later F-80) Shooting Star flies

June 6, 1944 Operation *Overlord*/D-Day

June 19–20, 1944 Battle of the Philippine Sea

July 12, 1944 Gloster Meteor I becomes first jet aircraft to enter operational service with the RAF

July 27, 1944 first combat sortie flown by Gloster Meteors, against V1 flying bombs

July 28, 1944 de Havilland Hornet flies

July 1944 Me 262 believed to have entered service

August 28, 1944 first loss of a jet aircraft (Me 262) in aerial combat

February 7, 1945 Consolidated XP-81 escort fighter becomes the first turboprop-powered aircraft to fly in the U.S.

February 21, 1945 Hawker Sea Fury flies

August 3, 1945 Kyushu J7W Shinden, a Japanese high-performance interceptor, the only production combat aircraft of canard configuration, flies

August 1945 Nakajima Kikka, the only Japanese turbojet-powered aircraft to take off under its own power in WWII, flies

August 1945 world's first atomic bombs dropped on Hiroshima, on August 6, and Nagasaki on August 9

August 15, 1945 2,257th and last sortie by a Japanese suicide aircraft

September 2, 1945 Pacific War ends

November 7, 1945 Gloster Meteor F.4 establishes a new world air speed record of 606.38 mph

December 3, 1945 de Havilland Vampire becomes world's first pure jet aircraft to operate from an aircraft carrier

September 7, 1946 Gloster Meteor F.4 increases world air speed record to 615.65 mph

April 24, 1946 MiG-29 and Yak-15, the first pure Soviet jet aircraft, fly for first time

May 15, 1946 first flight of the de Havilland DH108

June 7, 1946 Short Sturgeon prototype flies

June 22, 1946 first U.S. airmail to be carried by turbojet powered aircraft by a P-80 Shooting Star

July 21, 1946 McDonnell FH-1 Phantom becomes first U.S. pure jet aircraft to operate from a carrier

July 24, 1946 first recorded use of an ejection seat, made using a Martin-Baker ejection seat installed in a Gloster Meteor

August 17, 1946 first manned test of a U.S. ejection seat, from a Northrop P-61 Black Widow

June 17, 1947 Supermarine Attacker flies

June 19, 1947 Lockheed P-80R Shooting Star sets a new world air speed record of 623.61 mph

July 1947 McDonnell FH-1 Phantom first operational pure jets to operate from a carrier

July 16, 1947 first flight of the Saro SR.A/1 fighter flying-boat

August 20, 1947 Douglas D-558 Skystreak establishes a new world air speed record of 640.60 mph

August 25, 1947 Douglas D-558 Skystreak increases record to 650.78 mph

September 18, 1947 USAF comes into being

October 1, 1947 XP-86 Sabre flies

October 14, 1947 Bell X-1 first aircraft in the world to fly faster than the speed of sound, and sets a new Progressive Air-launched record of 700 mph

February 4, 1948 Douglas Skyrocket becomes first piloted aircraft to be flown at twice the speed of sound

March 23, 1948 de Havilland Vampire I establishes Progressive world absolute height record of 59,445 ft

April 25, 1948 XP-86 Sabre exceeds Mach 1 in a shallow dive

June 26, 1948 Berlin Airlift begins

July 14, 1948 first east-west crossing of the North Atlantic by turbojet-powered aircraft (Vampire F.3s)

August 16, 1948 Northrop XF-89 Scorpion flies

August 23, 1948 McDonnell XF-85 Goblin flies

September 1, 1948 Saab J-29 *Tunnan* (Barrel) becomes first European swept-wing jet fighter to enter operational service after WWII

September 6, 1948 F-86A sets a new unofficial world absolute speed record of 666 mph

September 1948 DH 108 first British jet-powered aircraft to exceed Mach 1

September 15, 1948 F-86A Sabre raises world air speed record to 670.84 mph

1949 NATO (North Atlantic Treaty Organization comes into being

April 21, 1949 first flight of French Leduc 0.10 experimental ramjet powered aircraft after release from a motherplane

September 4, 1949 first flight of Avro 707 delta-wing research aircraft

June 25, 1950 Korean War begins

September 22, 1950 first non-stop crossing of the North Atlantic by a turbojet fighter aircraft (EF-84E Thunderjet)

November 9, 1950 first USN jet to down another jet aircraft (F9F destroys a MiG-15)

December 17, 1950 first MiG destroyed by a Sabre in the Korean War

January 23, 1951 F4D-1 Skyray flies

June 20, 1951 first flight of Bell X-5

July 20, 1951 first flight of the Hawker Hunter

August 5, 1951 first flight of the Supermarine Swift

August 22, 1951 Supermarine Attacker enters service with FAA

November 26, 1951 first flight of the Gloster Javelin

January 4, 1951 Chinese and North Korean troops capture Seoul

November 2, 1952 first jet night kill, by a F3D-2 Skyknight shooting down a Yak-15.

October 20, 1952 first flight of the Douglas X-3 research aircraft

October 1952 Kenyan Emergency

November 3, 1952 first flight of Saab 32 Lansen all weather/night fighter

November 19, 1952 F-86D Sabre establishes a new world air speed record of 698.35 mph

November 22, 1952 F-84F Thunderstreak flies

December 8, 1952 Operation *Becher's Brook,* Sabres flown from Canada to UK

March 2, 1953 first flight of the Sud-Ouest SO 9000 Trident mixed power research aircraft

April 24, 1953 YF-100A prototype flies

April 9, 1953 first flight of the Convair Dart

April 30, 1953 F-86H flies

May 1953 F-86 Sabre becomes the first swept-wing fighter in the RAF

May 25, 1953 first flight of the YF-100A

July 16, 1953 F-86D sets a new world air speed record of 715.60 mph

July 22, 1953 last combat between MiG and Sabre in Korea

July 27, 1953 Armistice in Korean War

September 7, 1953 Hawker Hunter 3 sets a new world air speed record of 727.48 mph

September 25, 1953 Supermarine Swift 4 raises record to 735.54 mph

October 3, 1953 F4D-1 Skyray sets a new world air speed record of 752.78 mph

October 24, 1953 first flight of YF-102A Delta Dagger prototype

October 29, 1953 YF-100A Super Sabre sets a new world air speed record of 754.99 mph

November 1953 Douglas D-558-II Skyrocket sets a new Progressive air-launched record of 1,327.00 mph

December 12, 1953 Bell X-1A sets a new Progressive air-launched record of 1,612.00 mph

March 4, 1954 first XF-104 prototype flies

April 1, 1954 last operational sortie by a RAF Spitfire

July 30, 1954 first flight of the F11F-1 (F-11A) Tiger

August 4, 1954 first flight of the English Electric Lightning

September 1954 F-86Hs set new world speed records for the 500km and 100km closed circuits

October 6, 1954 first flights of the Fairey Delta 2 and F-8 Crusader

May 1955 Warsaw Pact, consisting of the Soviet Union, Bulgaria, Czechoslovakia, East Germany, Hungary, Poland and Romania formed

June 16, 1955 MiG-21 flies as Ye-4 prototype

August 20, 1955 F-100C sets a new world air speed record of 822.09 mph

October 22, 1955 first flight of the Republic F-105 Thunderchief

January 19, 1956 Supermarine Scimitar flies

February 17, 1956 First Flight of the YF-104A

March 10, 1956 Fairey FD.2 Delta sets a new world air speed record of 1131 76 mph

April 1956 F-102 Delta Dagger enters service

Early 1956 first flight of the Sukhoi T.3 (first of the Sukhoi family of Su-9/Su-11 "Fishpot" all-weather fighters)

April 30, 1956 first flight of the Sud-Ouest S.O.4050 Vautour II-A single-seat tactical fighter

September 27, 1956 Bell X-2 sets a new Progressive air launched record of 2094.00 mph

October 29, 1956 Suez Crisis

November 1956 Hungary invaded by Soviet forces

December 17, 1956 Dassault Mirage prototype IIIE flies

December 26, 1956 Convair F-106A Delta Dart flies

October 4, 1957 Sputnik I is first man-made satellite to enter an orbit around the earth

December 12, 1957 McDonnell F-10lA sets a new world speed record of 1207.34 mph

Apri 18, 1958 Fl1F-1 Tiger establishes a progressive world absolute height record of 76, 932 ft

May 7, 1958 F-104A establishes a progressive world absolute height record of 91,243 ft

May 16, 1958 F-104A sets a new world air speed record of 1403.79 mph

January 26, 1958 First production Starfighters issued to the USAF

November 25, 1958 English Electric P.1B prototype is first British aircraft to fly at Mach 2

March 18, 1959 Federal German Republic signs contract to begin license production of the F-104G

June 9, 1959 Republic F-105D all-weather fighter-bomber version flies

July 14, 1959 Sukhoi T431 establishes a progressive world absolute height record of 94,659 ft

October 1959 Last of F-100Ds built; 2,192 Super Sabres had been produced (**see picture, page 381 left, Royal Danish Air Force**)

October 31, 1959 Mikoyan Type Ye-66, a MiG-21 prototype, sets a world air speed record of 1,483.51 mph

December 6, 1959 McDonnell YF4H-1 sets a new absolute altitude record of 98,556 ft

December 14, 1959 F-104C establishes a progressive world absolute height record of 103,389 ft

December 15, 1959 F-106A sets a world air speed record of 1,525.93 mph

June 7, 1960 First flight of the F-104G

July 1960 English Electric Lightning enters operational RAF service

October 21, 1960 P1127 Kestrel VTOL aircraft makes first tethered hovering flight

1961 first flight of the Sukhoi T-58 (Su-15 "Flagon")

March 18, 1961 first flight of the Tupolev Tu-28-80 (Tupolev Tu-28 "Fiddler") long-range, all-weather interceptor

April 12, 1961 Flt Major Yuri Gagarin of the Soviet Union becomes first human in space

April 21, 1961 North American X-15A attains a speed of 3,074 mph

May 1, 1961 Francis Gary Powers, pilot of a U-2 spyplane, shot down by missile over the Soviet Union

May 5, 1961 Alan B. Shepard is first American to enter space

June 17, 1961 first flight of the HAL HF-24 Marut (wind spirit) single-seat ground-attack fighter, the first warplane designed and built in India

August 13, 1961 Erection of the Berlin Wall to divide East and West Berlin begins

September 1961 P1127 Kestrel VTOL aircraft makes first transition from vertical to horizontal flight

October 18, 1961 first USAF unit to operate from Vietnam

December 5, 1961 F-4 Phantom sets a new sustained altitude record of 66,443.8 ft

December 26, 1961 first USAF bombing mission of the Vietnam War

February 20, 1962 Lt John H. Glenn is first American to enter earth orbit

April 26, 1962 first flight of the Lockheed A-11 (later SR-71A)

July 7, 1962 Sukhoi Type E-166 sets a new world air speed record of 1665.89 mph

October-November 1962 Cuban Missile Crisis

February 29, 1964 existence of the Lockheed A-11 high altitude high-speed reconnaissance aircraft revealed

August 5, 1964 first F-4 combat sorties in Southeast Asia

1964 UK becomes the first F-4 Phantom export customer

September 9, 1964 Ye-155P interceptor (MiG-25 "Foxbat") prototype flies

December 21, 1964 first flight of the General Dynamics F-111A variable-geometry Mach 2+ fighter-bomber

March 6, 1965 first flight of the HAL Ajeet (invincible) an Indian version of the HS (Folland) Gnat

March 8, 1965 U.S. Marines land at Da Nang

April 9, 1965 first F-4 air combat victory (MiG-17)

May 1, 1965 Lockheed YF-12A sets a new world air speed record of 2070.10 mph

June 17, 1965 First officially confirmed USN victory over a North Vietnamese fighter (MiG-17)

July 10, 1965 First USAF air-to-air combat victories of the Vietnam War

September 6–27, 1965 Indo-Pakistan War

March 7, 1966 General Charles de Gaulle announces his intention to withdraw French forces from NATO

25 April 1966 MiG-21 seen for first time in Vietnam

December 23, 1966 Dassault Mirage F1C flies

December 27, 1966 Fiat G91Y prototype flies

February 8, 1967 first Saab Viggen prototype flies

June 5-10, 1967 Arab-Israeli Six Day War

October 3, 1967 X-15A-2 sets a new progressive air-launched record of 4,534.00 mph

August 23, 1968 McDonnell Douglas Phantoms enter service with the RAF

November 1, 1968 President Lyndon B. Johnson orders a halt to all bombing of North Vietnam

December 31, 1968 first flight of the world's first supersonic transport aircraft, the Soviet Union's Tupolev Tu-144

March 2, 1969 BAC/Aérospatiale Concorde makes first flight

April 28, 1969 RAF Harrier GR.1 makes first transatlantic crossing by the type

May 4–11, 1969 RN Phantom establishes the fastest overall west-east time in the Daily Mail Transatlantic Air Race

July 21, 1969 American astronaut Neil A. Armstrong first human to set foot on the moon

August 16, 1969 Darryl Greenamyer flying a modified Grumman F8F-2 Bearcat sets a new world air speed record for piston-engined aircraft of 477.98 mph

1969 Egyptian (Arab)-Israeli War of Attrition

1970 USMC withdraw from Vietnam
December 3–16, 1971 Indo-Pakistan War
May 10, 1972 Bombing of North Vietnam finally resumes with *Linebacker I* raids
May 1972 USMC F-4s move to Thailand to fly strikes against targets in Laos and North Vietnam
May 26, 1972 Soviet Union's Tupolev Tu-144 becomes first supersonic transport to exceed a speed of Mach 2
December 13, 1972 North Vietnamese negotiation delegation walk out of Paris Peace Talks with Henry Kissinger
December 18–29, 1972 *Linebacker II* all-out unrestricted air offensive by the USAF, USN and USMC in Vietnam
January 3, 1972 all U.S. bombing ceases above the 20th Parallel in Vietnam
January 8, 1973 137th and final USAF victory (MiG-21) in Southeast Asia
January 23, 1973 Cease-fire brings U.S. participation in Vietnam War to an end
October 6–22, 1973 Yom Kippur War; (though hostilities cease on Syrian-Israeli front, fighting continues on Egyptian-Israeli front until at least October 26)
January 20, 1974` first (unintentional) flight of the General Dynamics YF-16 lightweight fighter prototype, during ground tests at Edwards AFB
April 12, 1975 U.S. Embassy in Saigon evacuated during North Vietnamese spring offensive in South Vietnam

April 29–30, 1975 900 Americans in Saigon airlifted by the U.S. Navy to five carriers. Saigon falls and the South comes under North Vietnamese control
September 16, 1975 MiG-31 "Foxhound-A" long–range interceptor flies
January 21, 1976 BAC/Aérospatiale Concorde flies its first passenger service flight
July 4, 1976 rescue of hostages at Entebbe by Israeli special forces; 11 Ugandan Air Force MiGs destroyed during assault
July 28, 1976 SR-71A sets a new world air speed record of 2193.16 mph
March 10, 1978 Dassault Mirage 2000 flies
January 26, 1969 first European-built F-16As delivered
March 9, 1979 Dassault Mirage 4000 flies
June 18, 1979 first BAe Sea Harrier for service with Royal Navy handed over
October 25, 1979 5,068th and last McDonnell-built Phantom, an F-4E for Korea, delivered; (**see picture, F-4C, Vietnam 1967, below**)
December 1979 Soviet invasion of Afghanistan
September 1980 Iraq invades Iran
April 12–14, 1981 Robert L. Crippen, pilot of the Space Shuttle Orbiter *Columbia* breaks all records for space flight by a fixed wing craft with a speed of 16,600 mph at main engine cut-off. *Columbia* takes off under the power of its own engines and those of two jettisonable boosters and makes 37 orbits before completing re-entry to the earth's atmosphere
April 2–June 14, 1982 Falklands War

June 1982 Israeli forces invade Lebanon; F-4Es using anti-radiation missiles and bombs destroy the vast majority of Syrian SAM batteries in the Bekaa Valley

1983 USMC takes delivery of the first production AV-8B VTOL aircraft

September 1983 Korean Airlines' Boeing 747 shot down by a Sukhoi Su-15 "Flagon"

April 14–15, 1986 Operation *El Dorado Canyon*; U.S. F-11s and other aircraft attack "terrorist-related" targets in Libya

May 19, 1986 first flight of the BAe Hawk 200 single-seat, multi-role lightweight fighter

September 7, 1987 Lockheed Martin F-22 Raptor single-seat high-technology fighter flies

Early 1988 overall production contract for the initial purchase of 620 Eurofighter single-seat air combat fighter aircraft (now Eurofighter Typhoon), with a further option for 90 aircraft, signed by the NATO Eurofighter and Tornado Management Agency (NETMA)

August 25, 1989 first flight of the Taiwanese AIDC A-1 Ching-Kuo air defense fighter developed with General Dynamics under the Ying Yang (Soaring eagle) programme

November 9, 1989 Berlin wall comes down

November 10, 1988 Existence of the F-1117A Stealth, the first production combat type designed to exploit low-observable (LO) technology, (which had been flying secretly since 1983), officially revealed

December 20, 1989–January 1, 1990 Operation *Just Cause*, the invasion of Panama by U.S. forces

August 2, 1990 Iraqi forces invade Kuwait

August 7–December 1990 Operation *Desert Shield*

December 1990 German re-unification completed; former East German air force personnel and some aircraft integrated

January 16–17, 1991 Operation *Desert Storm* begins

February 27, 1991 Kuwait liberated

February 28, 1991 Cease-fire in the Gulf War

April 11, 1991 Gulf War officially ends

April 1991 Lockheed Martin F-22 Raptor wins the competitive evaluation with the Northrop/McDonnell Douglas YF-23 prototype

March 27, 1994 DA.1, first Eurofighter 2000 prototype completed in Germany flies

May 25, 1995 Following their refusal to give up their heavy weapons USAF F/A-18Ds, F-16s, EF-111As, Spanish EF-18s, a Dutch F-16 and a French Mirage attack a Serb ammunition dump in Bosnia; Further F-16 raids continue next day

August 30–September 1995 Operation *Deliberate Force* against Bosnian Serb military targets

November 1995 first flight of the McDonnell-Douglas (Boeing from 1997) F/A-18E Super Hornet

September 7, 1997 first flight of the Lockheed Martin F-22A Raptor

September 25, 1997 first flight of the Sukhoi S-37 Berkut (Royal Eagle) single-seat research and warplane technology demonstrator

October 1998–April 1999 Operation *Allied Force* operations against Yugoslav targets in Kosovo; an F-117 is lost on March 27, 1999

October 24, 2000 Lockheed Martin XF35A (Joint Strike Fighter (JSF) demonstrator flies

January 2001 first flight of the Mikoyan 1.42 (1.44) MFI multi-role tactical fighter, Russia's "fifth generation fighter"

September 11, 2001 terrorists fly two airliners into the World Trade Center in New York and into the Pentagon in Washington D.C.; a fourth airliner comes down outside Pittsburgh

October 7, 2001–March 2002 Operation *Enduring Freedom* against Taliban targets in Afghanistan

Late 2001 Lockheed Martin XF35A declared winner of the concept demonstration phase (CDP) in competition with the Boeing X-32A.

April 2002 Italian-, German-, and British-built IPA Eurofighter 2000 production aircraft all fly for first time

March 19, 2003 Operation *Iraqi Freedom*; second Gulf War begins with attacks on Baghdad

16 April 2003 CENTCOM officials declare end of major combat action in Iraq

2004 costs of the U.S. JSF development program are estimated to have risen to £200 billion, the largest weapons program in Pentagon history

Index to Fighter Images

Picture Credits

All photographs from Salamander archives or from the author's collection.
Martin Bowman: pp 14-21, 27, 31- 34, 52, 53, 54, 59, 92, 195, 198, 114, 245, 248, 253, 316, 318, 320-24, 330, 340, 34-345, 348, 351, 356, 359, 361, 364-365, 375. Richard E. Bagg: 36-37, 46. Graham Dinsdale 39. Tom Trower 60. Ian Cadwallader 70. Charles E. Brown 71. Roland Baker 80, 82, 87-88. Dick Bagg 86. Bob Haines 120-121. Alastair Aked 172-177. Brian Allchin 223, 226, 231, 234-235.
The author and publishers would like to thank the many organizations and individuals who have helped to provide pictures and information, among them Matthias Vogelsarg, *Aeronautica Militare Italiana*, Canadian Air Force, Canadair, Dassault, General Dynamics, Grumman History Center, Israeli Aircraft Industries, Lockheed-Martin, MoD, Rolls-Royce, Royal Danish Air Force, Royal Hellenic Air Force, Royal Navy, Saab, USAF, USN, USMC.